ACROSS THE DIVIDE

NAVIGATING THE DIGITAL
REVOLUTION AS A WOMAN,
ENTREPRENEUR AND CEO

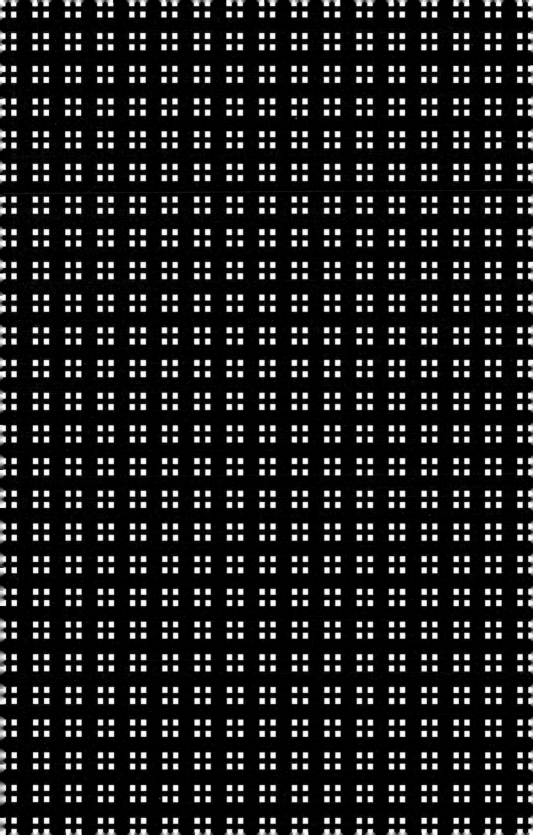

ACROSS
THE DIVIDE

NAVIGATING THE DIGITAL REVOLUTION AS A WOMAN, ENTREPRENEUR AND CEO

BY SUSAN S. ELLIOTT

Designed by Kiku Obata & Company

Edited by Casey Communications, Inc.

Published by Autobiographical
Publishing Company Pty Ltd

DEDICATION

ALL SSE EMPLOYEES

"A compelling history of information technology, one woman's drive for creating extraordinary value and sage advice for success in this very challenging economic world. A 'must read' understates the merits of this wonderful book."

General John W. Handy
USAF (retired)

"Across the Divide *describes a 50-year journey of epic proportions in technology, from the 1960s when transistor-tube computers filled spaces the size of football fields to widespread adoption of PCs in the 1980s and finally into today's world of web-based cloud computing. Passionate curiosity and total client-centered focus are Susan Elliott's constant companions as she built the technology company she founded and piloted through the rapids of change. The wins and perseverance are impressive and inspiring; the positive energy jumps off the page; and the intelligence and care with which she passes the baton of leadership to her daughter is certainly one of the greatest achievements of her richly-lived life."*

Gayle Jackson
President & CEO, Energy Global Inc.

"*Having built a remarkable 50-year career as a trailblazer in the IT industry, Susan Elliott is one of the most dynamic business leaders I know. Her experiences, set against the backdrop of the birth and maturity of the data processing – now information technology – industry combine to make up a truly extraordinary journey. Susan's motto – nothing as constant as change – has never been more relevant than it is now, and her ability to combine hard work with a nimble, entrepreneurial mindset serves as a model on how to survive and thrive in today's competitive business environment.*"

Ronald J. Kruszewski
Chairman and CEO, Stifel Nicolaus

Published in Australia in 2011 by
Autobiographical Publishing Company Pty Ltd
ACN 145 726 218

Autobiographical Publishing Company Pty Ltd
Reference Number: 987

National Library of Australia Cataloguing-in-Publication entry

Author:	Elliott, Susan S.
Title:	Across the Divide : Navigating the Digital Revolution as a Woman, Entrepreneur, and CEO/by Susan S. Elliott.
ISBN:	978 1 86470 455 6 (hbk.)
Notes:	Includes index.
Subjects:	Elliott, Susan S.
	Businesswomen--Biography.
	Women-owned business enterprises.
	Small business--Technological innovations.
	Office practice--Automation--History.
Dewey Number:	331.481004

Designed by Kiku Obata & Company
Edited by Casey Communications, Inc. and Linda Eardley
Published by Autobiographical Publishing Company Pty Ltd
Printed on 120gsm Sun Woodfree by Everbest Printing Co. Ltd., in Hong Kong/China

TABLE OF CONTENTS

INTRODUCTION

Throughout the years when I told people that I went to work for IBM as a programmer following graduation from Smith College in 1958, they would press me for more details. How did you happen to do that? How did you find out about such an opportunity? What was technology like in those days? Did you use punch cards? And then you started your own business; how and why did you do that? What was it like to be a woman in business way back then? After briefly describing the circumstances and reasons why, people would always respond with, "You should write a book."

The preparation for this book began in 2008 when SSE was planning a big celebration with our clients for 25 years in the PC world of business and 50 years for me in technology. Fortunately, I was a saver, and I plowed through old files, notes, Advisory Board agendas, strategic plans and speeches to develop a chronology of events. The purpose was to create panels of our history to be displayed at the celebration. We then had panels made that are displayed in our lobby in St. Louis.

As I fully transitioned the business to my daughter, Elizabeth Elliott Niedringhaus, during that same time period, she and I both looked for a project that would be meaningful for SSE. As this book endeavor became all-consuming, it did indeed "keep me out of her hair." In contemplating the real purpose of the book, other than documenting the history of SSE, my dream has been to "pay forward" all those extraordinary people, employees, advisors and friends who helped me along the way.

The stories and concepts in this book apply to entrepreneurs who might want to learn about how to start a business, understand critical success criteria, and anticipate the peaks and valleys of growing a business, including leadership succession. Business people, too, can compare notes about strategies and planning, focus, best practices and success criteria to manage growth and change in a privately-held business. And women may find encouragement and direction for pioneering and achieving success, whether or not they are striving in a man's world.

Lastly, as technology was the source and driver of our success, "old" techies may enjoy reminiscing about the origins and changes on the journey from Data Processing (DP) to Information Technology (IT). There is also relevance for "young" techies who want to understand the history of technology, Moore's Law, and the exponential pace of change and evolution since the 1950s. DP to IT reflects my mantra that there is "Nothing as constant as change!"

This book is an autobiography couched in the business experiences of a woman navigating in a man's world, pioneering in the digital revolution as it evolved from DP to IT. From my beginning with IBM out of college in 1958 as a programmer, I have thrived on breaking new ground for more than 50 years. The story evolves from getting the coveted job at IBM, being forced out of IBM eight years later because I was pregnant, founding my own business to keep working, launching an IT services business just after the first IBM PC came out in 1983 (undeterred by others' admonitions that PCs would never provide a solid business base) to building that business into a national player and ultimately effecting the unusual transition of President and CEO from mother to daughter.

This story about conceiving and running a business and managing exponential change in technology demonstrates how a small startup can and must grow. Anecdotes about attracting new clients, growing those relationships, planning and marketing strategically, and leadership succession provide insights for other entrepreneurs. The anecdotes share lessons learned, best practices and stories of leading-edge, first-ever business solutions, especially for recognizable, large corporate clients, along with a smattering of business planning and strategies for successful growth. The descriptions of many of our learning, application development and networking solutions, and how they contributed to the forward march of technology, demonstrate that passion for solving clients' business problems can drive success.

Further, this book is about a woman who believed that one would be rewarded for hard work and successful accomplishments rather than for entitlements just because she was a woman. There were, however, opportunities during those 50 years when organizations needed a token woman to serve on boards, both nonprofit and appointed. The story tells how those experiences became springboards to additional opportunities, including a pinnacle role on the Federal Reserve Bank of St. Louis board, first as Deputy Chairman and then two years as Chairman of the Board, during the Alan Greenspan years from 1996 through 2000.

The book concludes with a postscript from Elizabeth Elliott Niedringhaus, SSE President and CEO, that brings the SSE story to today. Clearly, by the time this is published there will be more changes in technology as we learned that there is "Nothing as constant as change." Changes in technology drove business opportunities to solve client problems, and our clients' needs drove our business to new heights, a virtuous circle!

We are blessed to have Elizabeth at the helm as she and her team will continue to tackle uncharted territory. The other two most important people in my life have been my husband, Howard Elliott, Jr., and our other daughter, Kathryn Elliott Love. Kathryn was the raison d'être that catapulted me into founding SSE and Howard has been my greatest support system throughout these 50 years.

— Susan S. Elliott

DP*
adventure
BEGINS

CHAPTER

1

"Isn't there a job somewhere in this country that doesn't require me to go to typing school after college?"

That was the question I posed to my college counselor as a senior in 1958 at Smith College in Northampton, Massachusetts, as most of my friends were getting married or choosing from the limited career options of the day: teachers, nurses or secretaries. I loved to work and a four-year degree from Smith, which in itself had been an awesome opportunity, had only whetted my appetite for tackling new frontiers.

There were seven Ivy League women's colleges at the time, and most of the men's colleges, such as Princeton and Yale, had not yet begun accepting women, nor would they until the 1970s. I had always heard of Vassar and Smith, both of which accepted me. Smith won my favor because of a camp counselor in Colorado during my early teens. I had great respect for her and knew she was a graduate of Smith. One did not visit the colleges for advance tours then, so the decision was very subjective. Six of us from my all-girls school, Mary Institute (now Mary Institute St. Louis Country Day School or MICDS) in St. Louis, Missouri, chose Smith, listed here by maiden name: the late Carolyn Cone, Terrie Corn, Elizabeth "Bess" Holmes, Esther "Estie" Veron, and the late Lois Weinstein. We packed our big trunks, boarded a train and arrived 24 hours later at Smith College to begin our exceptional four years.

That collegiate experience was a far cry from the small schoolhouse I attended for elementary school in St. Louis. When fourth grade work bored me, the teacher recommended that I skip to the fifth grade. With two grades in each room, I simply moved my desk across the room and was invigorated by new challenges. My love of work took me at age 14 to a downtown Clayton, Missouri, clothing store known as Gutman's. I counted inventory tickets torn off the price tags (in pre-computer days that is how retailers managed inventory), but I was too young to be paid so my work for two summers was for free.

The legacy of Headmaster Ronald Beasley at Mary Institute reinforced my desire to work when he told us, "You can go as far, as high and as wide as you want to. All you have to do is put your mind to it and do it!" I believed him and have repeated the encouragement many times since to my daughters and other young women.

■ ■ ■ ■ ■

In answer to my question about avoiding typing school, my college counselor revealed that IBM was actively recruiting women, and handed me an IBM brochure with violets on the cover. That stereotype-based marketing would likely draw a negative reaction today, but it was part of IBM's effort to recruit women and subsequently minorities. Ironically, my typing aversion led me into a world where keyboards were critical to communicating!

The college counselor told me IBM would test me for my analytical, logical aptitude, and if I passed, they would teach me everything I needed to know. I had always loved math, but there were too many other enticing courses and activities to merit holing up in my dorm solving deep math problems. Instead, I chose American Studies as my major, giving me the leeway to study every dimension

OPPOSITE Susan Spoehrer (later Elliott), then age 23, examining a card punched with holes representing letters and numbers that early computers could "read." St. Louis Globe-Democrat photo by Bob Briggs, 1961, used with permission of his family.

of America, art, history, philosophy, literature, religion, etc. In effect, it was a nondecision. My minor was psychology.

IBM testing showed I had the necessary aptitude, and I scheduled an interview in my hometown of St. Louis. It was unheard of then for a young woman to consider taking a job in a city such as New York and living in an apartment away from home. At my first interview I encountered resistance, being told I had not taken economics courses at Smith. I responded that I had had a whole semester to take such courses, yet IBM had not informed me economics was important; they backed off.

LEFT Massachusetts Senator John F. Kennedy spoke at the Smith College Commencement in 1958. Speaking with him are (left) Susan Spoehrer (later Elliott) and her good friend, Barbara Line Howenstine.
© Smith College Archives, Smith College. Photographer/creator unknown.

OPPOSITE The personal mantra of IBM Founder Thomas A. Watson, Sr., was reflected in the title of his biography by William Rodgers, published in 1974. All new IBM recruits received a sign for their desks that read, "Think."

IBM had a hiring freeze in the summer of 1958 because of a recession, so I did not get to go to work immediately. Subsequently, my father ran into the IBM Manager, Roy Plekenpol, in the Melbourne Hotel restaurant at Grand and Lindell boulevards in St. Louis' midtown area. It was just across the street from the IBM office, which was housed inside a former car showroom. My father told Roy of my continued interest. Finally, IBM hired me in July 1958 as a Systems Service Representative, a programmer position at a salary that didn't even top $1,000 a month.

That singular achievement marked the first step of my journey on a 50-year road in DP (Data Processing) that later became IT (Information Technology).

IBM *years*

IBM's "OJT" (On-the-Job Training) was truly the best preparation for business that anyone could hope to receive. In 1958, IBM had just decentralized its training from Endicott, New York, to its regional offices, so my basic training was in St. Louis. There were 11 weeks of classes from 8 a.m. to 5 p.m., Monday through Friday, with tons of homework each night. Every word was critical in the manuals we read as we trained for the extreme detail orientation of programming. To this day, it remains difficult for me to read without focusing on every single word.

Our training program concentrated just one week on computers, the 10th week. IBM's rationale was, " ... that is all anyone will need to know because there are not going to be that many [computers]." The other 10 weeks were focused on punched-card machines that we used for processing accounting applications, such as invoices and billing statements. Who would have ever predicted the changes that would occur over the ensuing 50 years!

Initially, we wired boards for accounting machines to read punched cards and print statements, invoices, reports, etc. My first IBM customer assignment was at Lewin Mathis Copper Refinery at 12th Street and Chouteau Avenue in St. Louis. I frequented the White Castle at 14th and Chouteau for quick lunches. We wore white gloves to work; some women wore hats. We sat in a big bullpen of gray desks. Men could smoke at their desks, but women were relegated to smoking in the ladies' room. Everyone sang "Ever Onward IBM" out of a hymnal at company events. When wives attended, the men with whom we worked daily avoided speaking to us.

My first experience on a computer was at Washington University in St. Louis in 1959 when I was 21 years old. Since our St. Louis office did not have a computer and Washington University had an IBM 650 computer in a Quonset hut on its main campus, I was invited to use the computer at 6 a.m. for a half hour to "play." I practiced coding routines, emulating what we were doing on the punched-card machines and "had a ball" learning how to use it. One tray of punched cards held 3,000 cards, and the ultimate disaster was accidentally overturning a tray while walking on the gravel streets to the parking lot. It did happen once and it was no small feat to pick up the cards from the gravel and clean off the dust so the cards were clean enough to go through the machine again!

That spring, I attended advanced classes in Chicago, including an Applications–Methods Class, March 30-April 17, 1959. I remember being so engrossed that I stayed up all night working on the machine while my male colleagues slept. The programming language was SOAP (Symbolic Optimal Assembly Program), and at one point I not only helped make some corrections to the code but also wrote additional code for the actual programming software, all of which was leading-edge at the time. Subsequently, my job title was changed to Systems Engineer and my role evolved from solely doing programming to more systems analysis and design, plus account responsibility.

With that "extensive" computer experience, I was assigned to Monsanto in 1960 to my first computer account. Our commitment was to develop and implement an order entry/inventory management initiative on the IBM 650 with

OPPOSITE Susan (seated) shows Mary Jane Kuefler how she "programmed" a job by flowcharting steps the computer followed to compute and solve problems. IBM's staff in St. Louis had 99 men and five young women. St. Louis Globe-Democrat photo by Bob Briggs, 1961, used with permission of his family.

which I was familiar, helping Monsanto programmers code the application. This was in the days when technical help came free to IBM customers with their equipment leases. Almost no mainframes were purchased outright until much later; and then they were generally purchased and leased back to the customer by a company such as Computer Sales International (now CSI Leasing, Inc.), whose technical support business we ultimately bought in 2001.

The IBM 650 was a vacuum-tube computer that took at least five minutes to warm up. It rested on raised floors with all the cables running underneath and a vast halcyon fire-protection system. The noise of the computer and the air-conditioning was so great that we yelled over the din to be heard. And when I returned home at night, my mother would remind me, "Sssh, I am right here next to you."

Monsanto was among the companies with corporate headquarters in St. Louis, as were Anheuser-Busch, Southwestern Bell and Emerson Electric, all of which were early technology adopters. IBM was the "only game in town in those days," as it had no real competition. Monsanto had previously acquired an IBM 702 for processing its other accounting systems data, thus the name "data processing." The 702 was the "old" workhorse and both Monsanto mainframes

BELOW The powerful vacuum tube used in the IBM 650 computer, which took at least five minutes to "warm up," was fodder for this cartoon. Reproduced from St. Louis Chapter Data Processing Management Association *TABLOID*, February 1964.

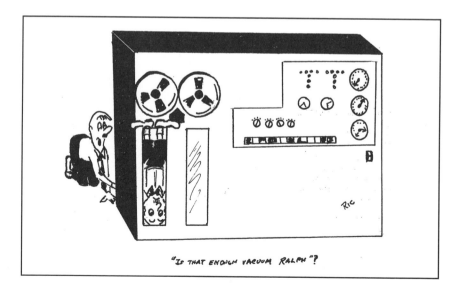

"Is that enough vacuum Ralph"?

were in a special computer environment in the basement of its C Building at its world headquarters campus at Olive and Lindbergh boulevards in Creve Coeur, a St. Louis suburb. Why they were numbered 650 and 702 (there was also a 701) remained internal to IBM manufacturing, as every IBM machine was dubbed with some sort of numeric or code identification.

One of the men I assisted on the order entry/inventory application programming assignment at Monsanto had a very difficult time working with a woman. I decided to confront the problem head-on and explained I was only there to help him shine with a successful application; I was not trying to compete with him. That direct approach helped and we worked closely thereafter. He even gave me a cigarette lighter that played "Smoke Gets in Your Eyes" for my birthday at a time when I fashionably smoked.

■ ■ ■ ■ ■

A year or so later, I remember sitting in a conference room at IBM and being told, "We are going to be able to search data randomly." Around the table, there was an audible, "WOW!" Talk about leading-edge technology, up until then all data was stored on tapes serially or in punched cards. To accomplish a search for a piece of data on tape required mounting the tape on a tape drive and reading the tape sequentially. Searching for "Taylor," for example, required passing through at least three-quarters of the tape to find the desired record in the Ts. This random data search breakthrough ultimately led to the development of programs that were called Information Retrieval (IR) applications. Those programs were the precursor to the ultimate IR application today, Google. Google's concept of entering a keyword to gather relevant information applies exactly the concept that we pioneered with IBM for Monsanto in 1961, nearly 50 years earlier.

Our Monsanto team was led by Senior IBM Account Representative Vince Petrea. I stayed on as a member of the team beyond the initial assignment and was privileged to play a major role in pioneering Information Retrieval for Monsanto's Chemical Research files with Steve Furth, an IBM specialist in New York. That project was driven by a need among Monsanto's research chemists and engineers to retrieve data from prior research projects and avoid the costs and delays of "reinventing the wheel." Quoting IBM Branch Manager Dalvin C. Tobin, "The objective was an efficient, accurate means of retrieving information contained in Monsanto's approximately 22,000 internal reports, dating back over 25 years. The immediate necessity was to replace the manually prepared abstracts with machineable records."

As a pilot to test the concept, Monsanto indexed its Chemical Economics Library of periodicals, under its Director of Libraries Paul Logue and librarian Jeanette Livasy. The pilot was implemented on an IBM 305 RAMAC, IBM's first random access device, and proved that more documents could be retrieved through a keyword search on the computer than the librarian could produce manually. Reminder: Google was not yet an apple in anyone's eye.

The RAMAC resembled a big Wurlitzer jukebox with platters of records spinning in milliseconds (MS), a speed we considered very fast. The read/write heads clicked up and down between the records to input and output the data. Programmers planned where each byte of data would reside and even programmed all input/output routines. We discovered the MS speed was not as swift as we had thought, so we turned to planning the placement of each category of data to reduce access time. For example, the customer name and address file was placed adjacent to the invoice file.

The pilot's success led Monsanto to embark on a program to deep-index its Technical Libraries using keywords. The critical words, keywords, in each document were flagged to identify the subject matter. The "deep" concept meant that keywords had to be assigned in great depth and specificity in order to accurately retrieve the applicable documents through a search.

Each document was valued at more than $10,000 by Monsanto, so the objective of quickly retrieving prior research information was enormous. Prior to that time, Monsanto scientists, unaware that certain research work had already been done, ended up duplicating the cost and time unless someone recalled and shared that the topic had been studied earlier. We implemented the new system on an IBM 1401, the generation of computers to follow the IBM 650. It was still driven by punched cards.

The project's biggest challenge was finding a way to handle the long chemical names, which would not fit in one 80-column card. An example was the 54-character CYCLO-PENTANEETHYLAMINE, N, A-DIMETHYL, HYDRO-CHLORIDE. The solution limited the chemical name to 32 columns in each card and then assigned a numeric coding structure to be punched in each of the cards so paired cards would be processed together. The number was the same in each card to keep them together, but an additional digit of 1, 2, 3, etc. was required to identify the proper card sequence.

The solution I conceived was subsequently recognized at the corporate level with selection of my technical paper for presentation at the first IBM Systems Engineering Symposium in Washington, D.C., in the fall of 1962. My paper described the method Monsanto adopted. It was defined as a numeric coding system, and the process was facilitated by a "tub file" approach. Essentially, punched cards that contained the key chemical names, keywords, upon which searches were to be conducted were pulled from the huge "tub files" of cards and entered into the computer. The computer then searched all the documents whose content had been flagged to identify a match on the chemical names in the punched cards. The automated search generated a list of all Monsanto library documents containing information about the specified chemical(s). With the computerized access to pertinent information, scientists were able to retrieve relevant prior research to avoid duplication and spur research advancement. This primitive process was the forerunner of, but a far cry from, search engines and the digital scans used by Google today for harvesting information.

The paper, *Index Preparation and Library Processing at Monsanto Chemical Company's Research Center*, published as an IBM Application Brief, was also requested by a principal in the Thomas J. Watson Research Center in Yorktown Heights, New York, to assist the IBM team there in the development of a relevant solution, *Removing Vowels to Conserve Storage Space.*

Clearly, my early involvement in application development projects at Monsanto, developing an order/entry application and, most especially, working to pioneer Information Retrieval, ranked as leading-edge efforts in the brave new world of computers. They also fueled my passion for solving clients' business problems with the latest and greatest technology. Truly, this was the beginning of a career in which I was blessed to be among the early initiators.

■ ■ ■ ■ ■

IBM continued to produce mainframes, introducing the System 360 in 1964 as the next major advancement in computer technology. Its processing speed was measured in microseconds and programming was done in the new programming language of COBOL (COmmon Business-Oriented Language), standardized four years later in 1968. COBOL attempted to mirror the English language more closely than other available options.

I was promoted to an IBM Advisory Systems Engineer in 1964, reflecting my increased emphasis on systems analysis and account responsibility. The timing of that move meant I never learned COBOL in the same depth that I had learned SOAP for the 650. This reinforced my transition to conceptually solving a client's business problems while relying on other technical experts to execute programming details.

Having completed work with Monsanto in 1963, I assumed account responsibilities for IBM at Brown Shoe Co. with Rich O'Neill, then at Anheuser-Busch (A-B) and lastly International Shoe in about 1965. In those days at A-B, coolers were always stocked with beer at the water fountains and employees could help themselves at will all day long.

During my stint at International Shoe, I found I was pregnant with our first child. Great news, but I then learned that IBM's policy (and that of many other companies) was to send women home when they were six months pregnant to "eat bonbons" and wait three months because they were so fragile. (Perhaps a filing cabinet drawer might open and hit them in the stomach!)

Not only did I love my work, but my husband, Howard, was just out of Washington University Law School in St. Louis and my income was important to us. We had married in 1961 before his last year of law school, and by 1966, he was still building a practice in his father's law firm, Boyle, Priest, Elliott and Weakley.

First National Bank in downtown St. Louis was eager to tap my IBM technical skills, but had the same maternity policy as IBM. So we made the big decision! Howard used his new legal expertise to incorporate my business, and the bank felt protected to contract with a corporation rather than hire a pregnant woman. Systems Service Enterprises, Inc. was born. Indeed, we turned the lemon of policies denying work to pregnant women into the lemonade of a new business!

OPPOSITE TOP Data was stored on rolls of magnetic tapes as well as punched cards. Susan mounts a roll onto the RAMAC 650 tape system at Monsanto Chemical Co. in St. Louis, where she was assigned to program the $500,000 random access computer to perform payroll, inventory and other jobs. In the foreground is a tractor feed printer on which green and white-striped paper was mounted. The 650 system rented for $14,000 per month and came with free technical assistance. BOTTOM Susan (standing, left) and IBM Systems Engineer Rich O'Neill (standing, right) meet with two data processing employees at Brown Shoe. *St. Louis Globe-Democrat* photos by Bob Briggs, 1961, used with permission of his family.

launching SSE

CHAPTER

3

Systems Service Enterprises, Inc., or SSE, was incorporated in the state of Missouri on March 8, 1966. The company name built upon my original IBM job title, Systems Service Representative, and the notion that "enterprises" would allow us to be whatever we wanted to be as we "grew up." The letters also happened to match my initials, Susan Spoehrer Elliott. I thought, "If International Business Machines can be IBM, then surely Systems Service Enterprises can be SSE!"

When I departed from IBM, my colleagues there, Martha Conzelman and Carol Stehlmach, planned a retirement lunch for me at the Cheshire Inn, a restaurant on the western edge of St. Louis. Everyone contributed toward a present, which was a lovely Steuben snail. It was wrapped in a huge box, and when I opened what looked to the men to be a tiny piece of glass, there was a perceptible whisper around the table. As the message traveled quietly from one person to the next, "Steuben snail" became "stupid snail." Later I learned the

Native American "animal medicine" associated with the snail is perseverance and determination, character traits that proved valuable to SSE's future success.

Our first child, Kathryn, came into our lives in June 1966 and I worked until the day before she was born, defying the then-current practice and setting an example for the future. I won consulting assignments on a freelance basis from 1966 until I fully revived SSE in 1983. Following my husband's appointment to the Missouri Public Service Commission in 1967 and our move to Missouri's capital in Jefferson City, I was hired for a project with the Missouri Department of Elementary and Secondary Education (DESE).

LEFT This hand-crafted sign was painted by Kathryn Elliott for the window of her mother's first basement office in 1983.

The state had used excess cash remaining at its fiscal year-end (June 30, 1967) to acquire an IBM 1410. It was a great idea as they had programmers to code for the computer, but no one on staff could perform the needs assessment, systems analysis and design of the requirements. I was fortunate to have contacted IBM friends in Jefferson City with whom I had worked in St. Louis who happened to know of DESE's needs. I was truly at the right place at the right time with the right skills, and was hired to design and work with three programmers to implement the state's first computerized Student Information System. The system gathered, recorded and tracked DESE public school classifications, and then confirmed that teachers were properly certified for their teaching assignments. That was followed by design and implementation of a school lunch program to ensure public schools statewide were serving the food prescribed for the school lunches.

Our second daughter, Elizabeth, was born in 1969, and we moved in late 1970 to Washington, D.C., when Howard was appointed by President Richard Nixon as one of the first five commissioners on the newly established U.S. Postal Rate Commission. As a semiautonomous corporation, the commission decided postage stamp rates, a function formerly performed by Congress. The commission's first big decision was to raise the cost of a stamp to eight cents!

Our family returned to St. Louis in 1973 when my husband accepted a position as associate general counsel at Laclede Gas Co. Though SSE was not active in the marketplace as I raised our children, I renewed SSE's corporate license annually with the explanation, "business temporarily suspended." It was important to me to keep my options open for the "enterprises" that might arise when I would re-enter the marketplace.

On our return, my "best buddies" from Mary Institute welcomed me back to St. Louis with open arms, including adding me to their weekly tennis game. In 1985, we lost Carol Jones Veron to cancer and we vowed after that not to let our friendships get lost with time, so we scheduled a lunch monthly that continues to this day. The group was five strong: Talbot Leland MacCarthy, Estie Veron Pruett, Mary Vollmer Rassieur, Almira "Mydie" Baldwin Sant and me. When Jane Cochran Hughes moved back to St. Louis in 2006 after being away for 50 years, we welcomed her into the fold.

■ ■ ■ ■ ■

In late 1979, I resumed my professional career at the same First National Bank in downtown St. Louis where I had won my first business contract in 1966 while pregnant. My daughters were then 10 and 13; and the 10-year-old was not happy, thinking I would not be accessible. In reality, I told her to think of this as what I "volunteered" to do because it was my desire to work; and working put me closer to a telephone than I would be if not working, since there were no cell phones then.

A friend, Clark Driemeyer, was aware through networking that I was looking for opportunities to return to technology, and also knew that my IBM expertise equipped me to oversee First National Bank's new system implementation. He introduced me to the decision-makers, and I was hired to work under Greg Kintz. His department was poised to implement a lease management system to administer leases of large equipment, such as barges and corporate aircraft, purchased for its customers and leased back to them. The bank purchased the specified assets, earning tax credits based on the U.S. Revenue Act of 1971 that permitted a 10 percent investment credit on qualified property.

The lease management software was written by Wells Fargo Bank in San Francisco and implemented on a large computer in Rockville, Maryland. Corporations could purchase the use of the software nationwide. This was an early application of the "cloud computing" of today. It was my first experience with data communications and receipt of data on a teletype-like terminal. After not working for nine years, I had to "dust away the cobwebs." Everything had changed. The work, another leading-edge experience, fueled the newest phase of my adventure in technology!

One dividend of my time at the bank was that I had lunch weekly with my father, Charles H. Spoehrer, at the Noonday Club. My office was on the 18th floor of the LaSalle Building adjacent to the bank, and the Noonday was one floor above. We had lunch in the room reserved for "men only," and the Noonday was distressed that my father was bringing his daughter into that room. Fortunately, Daddy ignored their warning to cease and desist; I treasured those lunches and the opportunity to spend such quality time together.

A series of other assignments followed at the bank, including an encounter with newly issued IBM Personal Computers (PCs) adopted by the bank's typing pool. IBM introduced its first PC on August 12, 1981, and soon captured 75 percent of the market, driving competitors to develop clones. I loved this exposure, but would never have dreamed of having one of my own. Yet that development propelled me directly into reviving SSE in 1983!

■ ■ ■ ■ ■

In the intervening 17 years (1966–1983), I had undertaken a number of commitments in nonprofit organizations and for the school my daughters attended, Mary Institute (my own alma mater). I served as President of its Alumnae Association, Vice Chairman of the Board of Directors and led the search for a new Head of School. I was also most active on the Visiting Nurse Association Board of Directors, ultimately becoming President of the Board in the early 1980s.

The combined experiences proved invaluable for learning how to lead people and organizations, and for gaining exposure to senior management and business operations. Successful leadership of volunteers portended that it was possible to work successfully with any group. From those experiences, I grasped that learning and developing as a leader could come from a multitude of different and unrelated experiences beyond running a business.

This realization led to a philosophy I have described as "Life is a Mosaic." We engage ourselves in experiences according to family situations and our needs at different times and places, and these random experiences shape the person we become and the capabilities we develop. When we then settle into what seems to be life's passion and commitment, the pieces of the mosaic fall into place and help ensure the success of the venture. My time away from full-time work had not been wasted in any regard.

One anecdote about delegation and leadership in those "mosaic" years: our daughter, Kathryn, turned 16, and had just received her driver's license in 1982, the day before her sister, Elizabeth, age 13, managed to fall off her bike while practicing "bike ballet." Elizabeth's arm hurt the next morning, so I said: "This is great; your sister can drive you to the doctor." Little did I suspect that her arm was broken in two places and the two girls would end up having to cope with the doctor rebreaking Elizabeth's arm and putting it in a cast. Not surprisingly, my daughters grew up with a great sense of independence and self-confidence!

■ ■ ■ ■ ■

Early in June 1983, my husband and I attended a charitable auction, held at McDonnell Douglas, then a dominant American aerospace company (later acquired by Boeing). En route to the event, while perusing the items to be auctioned that evening, I mused to Howard, "Can you imagine having a computer in your home?"

During the live auction, my husband raised his hand and we purchased our first PC for about $4,000. When our friend, the late Don Danforth, who had bid against Howard, asked what I planned to do with our new PC as we left that evening, I spontaneously said, "I am going to revive my business!"

I was so excited that it kept me awake all night. Not only did we have a computer for our home, unthinkable prior to that evening, but I was now equipped to propel SSE back into gear. I confess that when I attended my 25th reunion at Smith College earlier that summer, I had expressed my desire and was encouraged by my former classmates to get back to my business. Now I simply needed to give my notice at the bank and launch SSE full-time. What was termed Data Processing (DP) in 1958 had evolved to Information Technology (IT); and I was poised to resume business at the beginning of the PC and IT revolution! (See page 159 – PC Costs and Features in 1981 vs. 2001.)

When I told my father of my business revival plan at one of our weekly lunches and asked him to poke holes in my idea, he simply said, "Go for it! You can do it!"

SSE *embraces* the PC WORLD

CHAPTER

4

After three-and-a-half years back at Centerre (First National Bank had changed its name to Centerre in the early 1980s), I gave three weeks notice leading up to my last day on June 24, 1983. On Monday morning, June 27, I descended our basement steps for my first day of work and the beginning of my full-time commitment to SSE.

I remember donning a khaki skirt and blouse, just as if I were leaving home to go to work. The khaki attire was a far cry from the business suit of my IBM days, yet by "dressing" for work and going downstairs, I separated myself from the ever-present household chores. The only problem I remember is missing "drive time" to organize my thoughts.

My basement office measured 400 square feet. "Amenities" included concrete walls, a washer and dryer at one end of the room, a bare light bulb in the ceiling, and a desk, artfully constructed of a long piece of plywood stacked on two wooden horses. The auction-acquired PC that inspired my business relaunch sat on another piece of plywood atop two two-drawer

ABOVE When Susan launched SSE on June 27, 1983, SSE's furnishings and equipment included Susan's first IBM PC, purchased at an auction, situated atop a piece of plywood perched on two two-drawer filing cabinets. The 400-square-foot basement office had concrete walls, a bare light bulb in the ceiling and a window where SSE's wooden sign sat on the sill. *St. Louis Commerce Magazine* photo by Julie Dueber, November 1983.

filing cabinets with a hard wooden bench for seating, situated next to the Ping-Pong table.

The Ping-Pong table proved to be a key piece of furniture as we used it to assemble proposals. Unable to purchase letterhead stationery in a form suited for continuous feed printers, we devised a primitive solution with the stationery salesman. He supplied us with "continuous carrier" letterhead, single sheets of letterhead attached with rubber cement to continuous-form tractor-feed paper for printing on the dot-matrix printer. Then we carefully peeled each page off the form and scraped the rubber cement off the back.

Our daughters, by then aged 14 and 17, remember fondly (or not so fondly, at the time) calling down the clothes chute to beckon me upstairs to fix dinner. Howard was hard at work as an executive at Laclede Gas Co. and less directly impacted by the "new" office.

■ ■ ■ ■ ■

Famous-Barr (later Macy's), the department store that donated my PC to the benefit auction, offered training in how to use my new PC with its 160KB double-diskette drive. My half-hour lesson on how to program in BASIC (Beginners All purpose Symbolic Instruction Code) exhausted the salesman's knowledge. In addition to BASIC programming software, other software available at the time was dBASE, the first database language, and MicroPro's WordStar, the first word processor. WordStar initially had no spell-check feature. When that arrived six months later, we inserted a separate diskette in the drive to perform spell-checking.

Armed with my new PC "expertise," as opposed to my new IBM 650 expertise almost 25 years earlier, I was engaged by a good friend, Fred Hermann, to teach him and his two daughters how to use the IBM PC he had acquired at the same time Mary Institute purchased its first five PCs. I conducted classes in his upstairs study. Subsequently, he claimed that the training armed his daughter, Mary, to make a late application to Princeton and get an acceptance two weeks later. She had used the computer to generate her entire application!

Anecdotally, prospective clients would call and ask for help in "dBASE." We quickly learned this was the only name they knew and had nothing to do with what they really needed. Most often, they wanted to learn how to use the PC and perhaps install accounting system software.

■ ■ ■ ■ ■

To put this period in perspective, the IBM PCs introduced in late 1981 and early 1982 were loaded with DOS 1.0. Lotus 1-2-3, the first spreadsheet system developed for the IBM PC, was just beginning a $1 million advertising campaign. A million dollars seemed to be a staggering amount then to advertise software for a computer that would never be used in business. But it changed history. Lotus 1-2-3 became the most popular software on the market and was responsible for making the IBM PC the industry standard rather than Apple. (See page 160 – Great Moments in PC History.)

SSE's initial focus was helping small businesses make the right software and hardware decisions, and then assisting them with implementation to speed the learning curve. Our business model was patterned after the real estate office brokerage structure. I served as the marketing and administrative umbrella for a group of technical Independent Contractors (ICs), who delivered our services to clients. I chose to use the word "clients" instead of "customers" because I felt we were similar to a law firm, supporting clients' needs and building long-term relationships. No doubt this showed the subtle influence from my family of attorneys.

Since the revival of SSE was highly spontaneous and I had no business plan, I sought the help and advice of business and professional people whom I had admired through the years. They generously let me pick their brains as I probed different business opportunities associated with PCs and evaluated markets on which to focus. Many encouraged me to develop a niche right away, but my instinct was to keep my options open. At that time, no one anticipated the PC could be the driver of any business whatsoever!

SSE enjoyed a boost from my good friend, the late Ruth Krause Jacobson. She was the first female executive at Fleishman-Hillard, a St. Louis-based public relations firm, and offered to help SSE get some publicity. In conjunction with a good friend of my parents, *St. Louis Globe-Democrat* Publisher G. Duncan Bauman, an article was published entitled, "Entrepreneur Says Dream Came True," with a picture. The last paragraph quoted me as saying: "I'm very excited about the potential of my business ... I think the need is tremendous. The equipment is being sold, but there's a real need in helping people learn how to use it. That's what I hope to do."

The article produced new business inquiries and generated contacts from a number of potential employees excited by the prospect of working with a startup. Two of them came on board with SSE shortly thereafter: Jill Von Gruben, a housewife with small children who was anxious to get back to work, and John Y. Brown III, who was successfully employed at Monsanto but was a true techie at heart. Both were excited about getting in on the ground floor of the PC explosion.

FIRST FOCUS: CONSULTING THROUGH IBM

Another big step forward was achieved by reconnecting with my former friends at IBM. We became part of IBM's Marketing Assistance Program (MAP) for its new PC retail store, the Product Center, in downtown St. Louis at Broadway and Olive Street. The relationship produced a ready-made referral source for SSE and helped build a solid reputation. "Big Blue," IBM's well-known nickname from the color of its logo, was the trusted computer company of the day and the "safe choice" for hardware and software.

Business people who could finally afford an IBM product with the PC price tag would come into the store and ask the salesman what they should buy. (Clearly, there were no saleswomen at that time.) When the IBM salesman directed them to SSE for implementation assistance, no one thought to question the recommendation or request a reference. When IBM clones became an issue, some customers asked us on the side to switch to cheaper, non-IBM clones, but found our commitment to IBM impenetrable. SSE gave up some business by not compromising our integrity or loyalty.

As we worked with clients, our focus was on understanding the problems and opportunities each business was trying to solve or tap with this new PC technology. After each call on a prospective client, I dictated my thoughts and notes about the objectives and requirements into a proposal format I had developed. My Dictaphone would help me clear my head for the next call, sometimes five in a day. The Dictaphone was the antithesis of the new PC technology. It was paired with an old transcription machine from my father-in-law's law firm.

Jill Von Gruben, who had called after reading the *St. Louis Globe-Democrat* coverage, became SSE's first employee, working part-time to run the office and transcribe my draft proposals. The turnaround to complete each proposal was usually about 10 days because of prospects' schedules and other business commitments we juggled.

SECOND FOCUS: TRAINING PIONEER

We were poised to meet market demand as PC purchases skyrocketed in 1984. Besides business owners making purchases at the IBM Product Center, individuals who were techies, also known as "eager beavers," wanted to learn how to use these newfangled machines. Concurrently, Bettie Schwartz, an assistant superintendent of the Ladue School District, was buying IBM PCs to complement the district's existing Apples, TRS 80s and Commodore 64s. An entrepreneur at heart who wanted to validate her decision by making money for the district on the IBM PCs during nonschool hours, she asked me to consider designing a program of adult evening classes to serve these early adopters.

We brainstormed class content and format, determining that optimal class duration was three hours. A one-hour class was insufficient to introduce a new concept and provide the hands-on training for each student, equipped with his/her own PC. We also felt our new students, usually business people, would not take time for a traditional semester-long class. So we devised four three-hour class sessions, conducted in four weeks.

Our objective was to develop a curriculum and provide instructors for "How To Use" classes for DisplayWrite, WordStar and Lotus 1-2-3. The most popular class was "Introduction to the PC," which fostered a basic understanding of the new PC vocabulary: hardware, software, floppy disks, etc.

As long as four people registered, the course was a "go." Every time enrollment was one person short, my husband would sign up because we made more money holding the class than what it cost to enroll Howard. Quite to his surprise, he felt we really did a good job.

The evening learning program was called "HI-U." Class promotion by the Ladue School District in its quarterly newsletters capitalized on the image of Charlie Chaplin used in IBM's national advertising. It was a win-win-win combination because the costs were already incurred by the district, SSE could provide the sweat equity and the "eager beavers" coveted learning about how to use this revolutionary device. Not only did we achieve the solution to Bettie's business problem, but the success of the classes put us in the forefront of pioneering PC training that was the forerunner of today's world-class SSE eLearning. Bettie was masterful at developing "win-win" strategies, which contributed greatly to the effort's success and reinforced SSE's business model for mutually-rewarding relationships.

FAR LEFT IBM used the likeness of silent film star Charlie Chaplin to sell high tech PCs to the masses beginning in 1983. LEFT Susan and Bettie Schwartz, an assistant superintendent of the Ladue School District in St. Louis, carried the theme into promoting early "How to Use" evening classes called "HI-U." The program launched SSE's early expertise in PC training which later led to desktop support services.

In just six months, we began selling classes to companies rather than individuals. The Ladue School District and SSE reached out to St. Louis' largest corporations with letters describing the team effort of business and public education. The letters were cosigned by Bettie and me, and then I penned a note on each to the corporate leaders I personally knew. Those notes to "Augie," as in Anheuser-Busch CEO August Busch III, and "Chuck," as in Emerson Electric CEO Charles F. Knight, helped get our letters bucked down to the training directors of each company. In the case of Anheuser-Busch, our communication went to Dan Schoenekase. He was always solicitous, but never bought a class because he was loyal to Productivity Plus, a firm we eventually acquired in 1998.

One key class was scheduled by Graybar Electric for all of its top executives. Graybar CEO Jim Hoagland was the cheerleader, and we assigned extra instructors to ensure all students' learning success. "Smothering" them with attention applied my old IBM training. It must have worked because they came back to SSE for development of a leading-edge application 10 years later.

The corporate business reduced the Ladue School District's administrative burden by consolidating enrollments and payments from corporations rather than many individuals. It also paved the way to the next major SSE focus. By the end of 1984, one incredibly active year, SSE had initiated two key practices, both aimed at solving business problems and tapping leading-edge opportunities: consulting on technology and PC training. We also stood at the brink of discovering the value of our technical support services to clients. These milestones coincided with investment in our first hard drive PC with 10 megabytes, a huge event!

THIRD FOCUS: LARGE-SCALE DESKTOP SUPPORT

With little time to catch our breath in 1985, and with PC sales to individuals slowing due to saturation (though saturation was clearly miniscule compared to what we know today), we shifted our main focus from small businesses and individuals to emphasize the sale of our services to large corporations. Big businesses were beginning to install PCs on employees' desks and needed to train groups of employees.

The big news was that PC purchases by the large corporations spawned a new service for SSE: installation of PCs on the desktop along with "over the shoulder" support for the users. Mary Berthold, our good friend at Monsanto, asked if we could unbox the PCs and install them on the employees' desktops. Since this was the first instance of a large-scale PC installation in a corporate environment, we briefly scratched our heads and decided we could do that. David Boudinet, a college student working part-time for us, took the assignment and the rest is history.

Initially, it was a natural step to provide our instructors to deliver personalized support at the desktop. One SSE instructor could support about 100 users. Pioneering a new consulting service in the tech world, Desktop Support Services, also helped SSE evolve from that first opportunity with Monsanto in 1985 to deliver network services as networks emerged in the early 1990s. SSE developed this niche further with our SSE + 911 Help Desk and, by 2006, with SSE's Pretecht managed services network support for small and midsize businesses.

DIVERTED FOCUS: LESSON LEARNED

Having developed a strong presence in the market for PC consulting and training support, we felt our next logical initiative was to join the midrange rendition of IBM's Marketing Assistance Program (MAP). Structured similarly to the MAP program in which we participated during IBM's retail PC rollout that gave SSE a kick-start, this was aimed at IBM's new System 36-38 midrange computers. The opportunity seemed promising. Corporations had begun migrating from mainframes to minihardware, and we reinforced our valuable relationship with IBM. IBM's competitors in the minicomputer field included Digital Equipment Corp.'s (DEC) VAX models, among others.

The move also was a way to get firsthand technical and customer service training since IBM offered free seminars to its partners. One of the best workshops IBM offered was on sales and "customer sat[isfaction]." A key message was that you had to gain the prospect's confidence within the first few minutes to establish credibility, or you could lose the prospect's attention. It taught me to add to my personal introductions that I was at IBM for eight years and an Advisory Systems Engineer. It always worked! At the final phase of the sales cycle, they taught us the last question to ask a prospective customer before seeking to close the sale. It was the only question for which a "no" answer was a positive response: "Is there anything else you need from us to make a decision?"

The big lesson we learned in hindsight was that trying to support the System 36-38 midrange computers was a distraction from our work with PCs, and counterproductive to the PC success we had achieved to date. Each time we tested the fringes of our expertise, we learned again to focus exclusively on PCs.

While I had not wanted to be forced into a narrow niche initially, it became clear by 1985 that our PC expertise was our greatest strength, and merited our total focus. PCs gave us a sufficiently broad band to incorporate consulting, training and support, yet were also specific enough to satisfy our yen for developing deep technological expertise.

Maintaining our focus on multiple aspects of PCs through the years subsequently helped navigate the peaks and valleys associated with cyclical client needs. When training needs slowed, tech support demand accelerated.

Although large corporations were shifting to midrange computers for their key data processing and corporate computing needs, PCs were not yet the computers of choice for the heavy lifting. PCs were widely accepted for desktop use, but it was the emergence of networks around 1993 and then client/server technology later in the 1990s that drove businesses to use PCs as the key technology they could trust to run their businesses.

EXTERNAL FOCUS: CIVIC ENGAGEMENTS

Building on the public service commitment of my husband, my parents and in-laws, I was invited to serve on the St. Louis County Civil Service Commission and then was appointed in 1985 by Missouri Governor John Ashcroft to a two-year term on the newly created Missouri Lottery Commission. The origin of these appointments was not tied to my own political involvement, but to my husband's. I was tapped either as a token woman or for my technology expertise. While these outreach and networking opportunities were indeed affirming, they also, more importantly, gave me greater exposure to the community at large.

One of the early tasks of the Lottery Commission was to choose the hardware and software to manage the lottery, which ultimately launched on January 20, 1986, with the instant game, Jackpot '86. As the lone technology expert among the three commissioners, I knew only too well that it was important to acquire systems that had been tried and proven reliable by other states. A newcomer to the market, however, offered the state a very low rate to get its foot in the door. I was adamantly opposed to selecting the untried system, but the state had to take the lowest bid. Two years later, after I had concluded my term, the Lottery Commission sued the software company and switched to the one we had recommended initially.

CORPORATE GIANT *takes chance* on **SSE**

CHAPTER

5

Within two years of SSE's launch, we saw a clear trend. The demands of large corporate clients aligned perfectly with our passion and talent for solving business problems with leading-edge technology.

EMERSON ELECTRIC SELECTS SSE

In July 1985, at the start of SSE's third year in business, Emerson Electric became the first large corporation to take a chance on SSE. Emerson was one of the top world headquarters companies in St. Louis and had learned of SSE through the letters we sent from the Ladue School District.

Emerson had selected Enable, a software system that combined word processing, spreadsheet and database capabilities, as the standard for its corporate headquarters. Emerson promised to award its entire training business to SSE if we could write courseware for teaching the software to their people in lieu of the expensive trainer they flew in from New York. Martha Conzelman, with whom I had worked at

IBM and recruited to serve as one of SSE's first instructors at Ladue, attended a class at Emerson taught by the New York instructor. She wrote the courseware, taught the course and earned for us the right to continue as Emerson's exclusive provider. Enable, developed by Enable Software Co. of Ballston Lake, New York, never caught on in the market and ultimately faded away.

Emerson became a great reference and signaled tremendous credibility for SSE in the corporate world. Their commitment brought with it the convergence of a need as well as a limitation: Emerson's executive-level employees could only get away from the office a few at a time during the day, but the Ladue School District could not spare the time slots they needed. We concluded that teaching at a location of our own would save travel time for us, eliminate the rental fee we paid to the Ladue district and, most importantly, better serve our new client. Emerson not only kick-started our corporate training business, but also helped to cost-justify a "real" office.

A REAL OFFICE

By then our basement office had grown to five desks with five computers and a conference table. When a job interview, a meeting and a telephone conference call all coincided one late afternoon, I knew we had outgrown our 400-square-foot space.

If that wasn't enough of a driver, the killer was that we lost a corporate business opportunity due to our unimpressive "premises." (I always had to chuckle that our first Dunn's report, sent to me unsolicited, said "premises orderly.") One day during pouring rain, a representative from Union Pacific had to slog across stepping-stones at the back of our house to get to our basement entrance, and he was not happy. Even so, our time would come. I had read in *INC. Magazine,* my bible at the time, that " ... [the] sin was not in losing a piece of business, but rather in not winning it back." How sweet it was to get what ranked then as the biggest project awarded to SSE from Union Pacific Technologies in January 1988.

Over Labor Day weekend in 1985, we moved into our first "real" office at 989 Gardenview Office Parkway. At 1,200 square feet, it was three times the size of our basement office and rented for $1,000 per month. The space had been used by a developer as his office, so it was outfitted with leftovers from his many projects to save money. One office had a sliding glass door, wallpaper was different in each room and two bathrooms were situated in the center of the space. With the excitement of the big move, we didn't notice those downsides.

We were most enthralled by the fact that we now had our own classroom with three PCs to do daytime training. The classroom was in a walled-off corner on a raised ledge with a fireplace, and three PCs fit perfectly. Don Streett, a friend and partner at Brown Brothers Harriman at that time, attended a session and praised the training, but declared the chairs uncomfortable. He was correct.

Our official office space and the financial commitment it represented proved to clients and prospects that SSE had expanded beyond a cottage industry and our 1983 revival was not the whim of a woman still tied to the home front. SSE was in business for the long haul!

GROWTH drives INTERNAL FIRSTS

Our success in securing Emerson Electric as our first corporate client underscored the need to tend to our own affairs, centering internally on strategy and planning to manage our growth successfully. Spring vacation, while the rest of the family played, was my thinking and planning time, the rarest of commodities to come by while I was wearing all the hats as the only manager.

As a company that had been driven most by the joy of solving client problems with technology, SSE needed to address the art and science of our own business and internal economics. Our first business plan, focusing on our goals and direction, included:

- The "minicomputer" still seemed to be a viable option. It was only later that it came to represent a hard lesson learned.
- Attention to "properly matching the appropriate technological solution to the individual client's needs" was a touchstone from the beginning.

- "Highest quality talent" and "state-of-the-art technology" were priorities from day one. Independent Contractors (ICs) remained our preferred employment approach.
- We felt equally well-suited to clients ranging from small businesses to large corporations.
- Our industry was still called "DP," Data Processing. The "IT," Information Technology, revolution had not yet occurred.

We also set out to:
- Refine pricing schedules to maximize profit margins, considering:
  - Pricing strategy
  - Independent Contractor reimbursement strategy
  - Incentive strategies based on market volume
- Implement methods to smooth and optimize cash flow, including:
  - Efficient client billing procedures
  - Establishment and use of a line of credit

The signature message from all our planning was summarized in one brief paragraph at the conclusion of SSE's 1986 business plan and guided what would become substantial efforts to map and create our future as a business.

"SSE, Inc. expects to provide the highest quality consulting and training service available in the Metropolitan St. Louis area and be the premier such organization with no peers."

With this initial business planning completed and the examples of business operations learned from our clients, 1986 became a year of many firsts. We embarked on several ambitious goals:
- Expand our full-time staff with a Vice President – Finance and Technical Services
- Create an Advisory Board, a group formed to listen, advise and help us grow
- Hire our first two marketing consultants
- Hire our first full-time technical employee as a member of our staff rather than as an Independent Contractor
- Hire our first recruiter
- Develop our first marketing plan that defined specific sales goals

BEGINNING AN EXECUTIVE TEAM

Just about when the strictures of our basement office were bursting, I began to realize that I was stretched entirely too thin and needed to expand my own capacity. It seemed SSE would collapse from its own weight without help. My business reading had made me keenly aware of the disappointments that came when entrepreneurs failed to learn the art of staffing for growth and effective delegation. I analyzed SSE's needs as follows:

- Deliver the highest quality services.
- Stay technically competent to be at the forefront, since the changing nature of the technology business was already apparent.
- Count on others for technical expertise and apply my skills to marketing and business leadership.
- Match the decision-making process to my collaborative style for sharing ideas, knowing one person can't have all the answers.
- Achieve profitable growth by focusing on financials, especially pricing and margins between gross revenues and Independent Contractor (IC) rates.

This analysis led me to invite John Y. "JY" Brown III to join SSE full-time as my business partner. He asked: "Why me?" I responded instantaneously. He was a known resource, as he had developed courseware and taught for us at night at Ladue School. He also was perfectly suited for SSE's needs with 18 years at Monsanto in DP and then in corporate finance. He had his MBA, and besides he was a male, which at the time seemed important to demonstrate that gender did not matter and that we were not just a group of females. Throughout the years, the best expertise and fit in our culture were the only hiring determinants.

JY shared my commitment to the concept of a technology services business, and we spent six months devoted to growing the business so we could afford him and test our compatibility for working together. He moonlighted each evening after his full-time work at Monsanto, assuming technical responsibility for a variety of issues.

JY joined SSE at the beginning of our fiscal year in March 1986 in the role of Vice President – Finance and Technical Services. Much to my husband's chagrin, JY's market rate salary postponed any salary for me for another year or so. We were fortunate my husband had a good job himself, so we could manage the situation until the business grew according to plan.

ADVISORY BOARD FORMED

The 1986 launch of our first SSE Advisory Board marked a significant turning point. The board gave me access to brilliant business people who listened to a fledgling entrepreneur and generously shared advice that helped us grow. I promised them only four meetings a year and no homework (no director fees either, just a gift of appreciation during the holidays). They were a conscientious group and in succeeding years, they requested financials in advance for prestudy. We were able to discuss critical issues aimed at building SSE's visibility and driving growth in the St. Louis community, guided by solid business principles.

There is no doubt that our Advisory Board was critically important to our startup success. Almost as valuable as the counsel, discussions and community outreach provided by each member, was the need to prepare quarterly financials for board members' review. That discipline and preparation required analysis and understanding of the components that were driving our growth and success.

Even if we had never held a meeting, we had done our homework, a process not followed by most small businesses.

The first board members included Mary Berthold in DP at Monsanto; Derick Driemeyer, Asset Management Division Founder at A.G. Edwards; AAA Missouri CEO Jim O'Flynn; Schnuck Markets CEO Ed Schnuck; and Virginia Weldon, MD, formerly Vice President at Washington University Medical Center and then Public Policy Executive at Monsanto. Tom Boudinet, in sales at IBM, also served on the board but resigned to avoid any conflict of interest when his wife, Jan, became one of our IC instructors and then their son, David, joined us part-time to deliver our first Desktop Support Services.

Ed Schnuck never made a meeting because of his advancing cancer and he passed away in February 1987, but his encouragement was lasting. One fond memory dates to 1983. He and I were talking at Mary Institute, on whose board we both served, he as Chairman. As I was telling him about reviving SSE, he said that his secret to time management was to make a list of people he had to call, along with their phone numbers, so that even if he only had a short time, he could get all his calls accomplished. He saved time by making the list at the end of each day for the next day.

Jim O'Flynn saw to it that I was appointed in 1986 to the AAA Missouri Board on whose Executive Committee I served until it merged with AAA California in 2008. Armand Stalnaker, former Chairman of General American Life Insurance Co., joined us in 1987, followed in 1989 by Paulo Products CEO Frank Rassieur and Terry Franc, Founder of Bridge Information Systems (later Thomson Reuters). Joe Smith, IBM Regional Sales Manager, joined after he retired from IBM in 1990, as did Tony Fruhauf, Head of School at Mary Institute, who was only with us for a short time, but was very helpful in the training arena.

One memorable opportunity provided by Armand Stalnaker was to speak to his class at the Olin School of Business at Washington University in St. Louis in February 1989. The chosen topic was, "What is the major strategic or policy decision in your firm?" The week prior to my presentation, John McDonnell, then CEO of McDonnell Douglas, discussed how critical it was to get their strategic plans right before committing hundreds of millions of dollars to designing and building a new plane.

The next week, I followed with a discussion on the other end of the spectrum: How to increase application development services to represent two-thirds of SSE's gross revenues, or about $3 million, by 1991. One of the foils for the overhead projector from the presentation said (in a kind of shorthand):

"If to be a company of choice (for the large corporations), have to be full-service company. If full-service company, have to provide consulting, systems and programming, as well as training services. Training services will diminish as we know them today."

I commented that I knew I was supposed to speak about a major policy decision that could be analyzed retrospectively, but I decided this was so critical to SSE that I would put myself through the analytical discipline while preparing for the speech. In fact, my position changed as a result of the analysis, which should reflect a lesson learned for the students about the importance of the process, and noted, "So you are tuned in on a current topic and making history with SSE."

Joe Smith, the friend and neighbor who later became an SSE Advisory Board member when he retired from IBM, provided an opportunity for outreach and visibility before the Clayton Rotary Club in 1986. Following is an excerpt from my introductory remarks:

"Many of you may have seen the cover of the May 26th issue of *Fortune Magazine* that is entitled, 'Puny Payoff from Office Computers.' I thought about this as a title for my remarks today and decided, at the very least, it is provocative, and at best, surely there is food for thought in the article. Furthermore, I would like to suggest that to learn from the article is to be able to derive a formula 'for a profitable payoff' from office computers."

My speech covered how to do a PC implementation correctly. Paul Strossman, a consultant who formerly had been Vice President of an Information Product Group at Xerox, was quoted by *Fortune* as saying: "Automate only after you simplify ... [Anticipate that the learning curve will be slow and lengthy] as getting there takes time." I covered several other key steps, which remain important today:

- Pay proper attention to needs and requirements, the first and most important step.

- Determine the hardware and software choices *after* the needs assessment is complete.
- Engage all the people in the organization in the transition.

I predicted that PCs would be bought for the home only when people could manage their personal finances or other meaningful applications became available. Essentially, the PC was too expensive and too much trouble to install just for recipes. The game-changing software of Quicken, developed by Intuit, Inc., was among the first to come on the market for home finances. By 1990, we were using Quicken Version 4.0 for DOS at home, and converted to Quicken for Windows in 1991, both delivered on 3.5-inch diskette drives.

When launching the Windows version, Quicken President Scott Cook boasted: " ... fun-to-use automatic data entry features that slash typing time ... QuickFill finishes the entry for you ... just tell Quicken when, and how often, a bill is due ... and it is paid for you automatically." How leading-edge was that! Quicken did indeed drive purchases of home PCs and, with Version 2011 available, still is going strong.

WANTED: MARKETING HELP

It became clear by midyear 1986 that we needed to become proactive, not reactive, in generating business. The days of waiting for referrals from IBM's retail operations were over. That called for expanding my own calling efforts, and I quickly recognized, as I had in bringing JY on the team for operations, that I needed marketing assistance as well.

Accordingly, we hired Lori Lewis as our first Marketing Consultant or MC, borrowing a title from IBM which implied something less hard-driving than conveyed by the title of salesperson. One of Lori's most successful tactics was that of "verbally taking a sale away" from a prospect when there was hesitance about signing on the dotted line. They would always reel her back in and give us their business.

Soon after, Tom Boudinet introduced us to Patti Harty, whom we added for $25 an hour to teach Displaywriter to an out-of-town client, similar to her role at Southwestern Bell Telecom before leaving to have her second child. She was excited about learning PC programming since she had always loved math and logic, so JY gave her an R:BASE book to take home, read over the weekend, and return with the design of an order entry and billing system. She returned on Monday from her less than inspiring weekend assignment and asked to be in sales, so she became our second MC in 1987.

As a former IBMer prior to her stint at Southwestern Bell Telecom, Patti focused on large corporations, and Lori concentrated on small businesses. We reinforced the importance of MCs in our 1988 Three-Year Strategic Plan, which outlined our intention to market and promote services through:

- MCs who will continue to be the primary mechanism for generating business as well as market research, visibility and awareness
- Supplemental, appropriate advertising and public relations; SSE will continue to seek opportunities for free PR (public relations) whenever possible
- Marketing manager needed when MCs exceed five to six in number

Patti recalled a lesson we learned the hard way. When she encountered resistance about our next training engagements at Monsanto from a new head of the training function, we strategized that I could contact someone I knew because "we had nothing to lose." The lesson learned: We upset the apple cart by going over the contact's head to higher-ups, and lost the business altogether.

IN-HOUSE TECHNICAL SUPPORT

Until the late 1980s, we delivered our technical services through our well-developed network of independent contractors. As we considered ways to build the best long-term client relationships, we decided one way to do this was to anchor the technical expertise of our ICs with a full-time resource on our payroll, and hired our first technical employee.

The addition enabled us to respond more rapidly to a crisis and ask questions later. It also gave us newfound discretion over providing some nonbillable services, not an easy proposition with an IC. The support we were able to give to clients helped retain them over time, even while a hidden benefit for us was that we achieved better margins as long as we could keep our employee busy.

Although in-house technical expertise became a necessity, there is no doubt that initially using ICs rather than fixed staff to deliver technical services was our second reason (the other being our Advisory Board) for a successful beginning.

Our contract with the ICs established that they would be paid within three days of SSE getting paid, so ICs took ownership of ensuring we had a totally satisfied client. We even did a joint goal-setting and objectives session each year with our ICs, so they felt they had "skin in the game" with our mutual client relationships. Obviously, this approach also helped manage our cash flow.

The concept of "smothering" our clients with care and attention was in play from day one. Knowing that bad news always travels faster and lasts longer than good news, our approach kept reputation-harming experiences from happening. Ultimate "customer sat[isfaction]" guided all we did to "provide the highest quality consulting and training service available ... and to be the premier such organization with no peers."

FIRST RECRUITER

We continued to attract self-starters to SSE. When Terry Sibbitts came into our office one day in 1986 and announced that we needed her, I listened. She had been doing research on St. Louis businesses in preparation for moving back from Chicago, and determined we needed her to recruit, interview and check references for the technical talent we needed.

It was a new concept to me, and heaven-sent. Our hiring of Terry as our part-time staffing manager not only relieved me of recruiting demands, but also leveraged her expertise in recruiting to benefit SSE and our clients. It was one more opportunity to take the "weight off my shoulders." Without her, we would have risked being ill-prepared for our impending growth.

Having just achieved the $1 million annual revenue mark, our growth expectations articulated in the FY1989 Three-Year Strategic Plan indicated ambitious but doable objectives:

- At least 100 people in combination of employees and ICs, with a greater ratio of employees to ICs
- $5 million to $7 million in revenues and 20 percent margin on revenues

In transitioning recruitment to Terry, I recognized the importance of a thorough selection process. I was fortunate to have learned key interviewing techniques when I led the Head of School search for Mary Institute. After key people in our organization interviewed candidates to confirm they met the needed qualifications, I interviewed each candidate to ensure a solid fit with our culture.

I always told them: "It is important for both of us that a job with SSE is a good fit; otherwise, let's not waste each other's time." To this day, many of our employees report that having a chance to meet and hear SSE's story from the founder's mouth was pivotal in their decision to join SSE.

CREATING A MARKETING PLAN

As the final step in our year of "firsts," we created our first marketing plan and established specific sales goals. It is special to note several items:

- We used flip charts. Next we used VideoShow for presentations, the precursor to PowerPoint that we take for granted today. As a point of interest, we created Emerson's Annual Board of Directors meeting presentations in VideoShow for several years.
- We recognized that technology was continually changing and it was critical to stay at the forefront.
- Dot matrix printing had its limitations!

■ ■ ■ ■ ■

We decided to focus on building one more large corporate relationship similar to the one we enjoyed with Emerson to avoid having all our eggs in one basket. That choice was Monsanto, whose culture favored outsourcing. Monsanto was also a natural target due to JY's many contacts there.

We succeeded. Monsanto engaged SSE to run the training for its Agriculture (Ag) Division. Martha Conzelman led the team and we acted as if we were Monsanto employees since Ag was reluctant to let it be known they were using outsiders.

After Monsanto, most of the large corporations in St. Louis engaged SSE at one time or another, including Anheuser-Busch, Southwestern Bell Corp. (now AT&T), Ralston Purina (now Nestlé Purina PetCare Co.), Enterprise Rent-A-Car, most of the banks and others. The courses typically concentrated on "What is a PC?," MultiMate and IBM's DisplayWrite (both word processors) and Lotus 1-2-3. In the late 1980s and early 1990s, WordPerfect was the word processor of choice. But in the 1993-1995 time frame, Microsoft emerged as the powerhouse with Word and Excel, totally outstripping WordPerfect and Lotus in popularity and sales.

```
┌─────────────────────────────────────────────────────────────────┐
│                                                                   │
│                        Flip Chart 8                               │
│                                                                   │
│                      Major Challenges                             │
│                                                                   │
│     o    Turn revenues into profits                               │
│                                                                   │
│     o    Develop visibility with limited resources                │
│                                                                   │
│     o    Stay in forefront of information revolution              │
│                                                                   │
│     o    Manage growth                                            │
│                                                                   │
│          —    Fiscal                                              │
│                                                                   │
│          —    Human resources                                     │
│                                                                   │
│                                                                   │
└─────────────────────────────────────────────────────────────────┘
```

ABOVE In the days before PowerPoint, flip charts and overheads were the standard tools of presentations. This 1988 flip chart, still produced on a dot matrix printer, recognized the ongoing challenge of staying in the forefront of the technology revolution.

Every new version of software was a boon for us, creating surges in training demands. Corporations typically shifted their training to in-house resources within three to four years as mastery of software penetrated their organizations. Thankfully, they came right back to us for more training when the newest software version was released.

A letter from Monsanto Information Systems Manager T.R. Tucker was of particular note: "The Personal Computer Overview class ... I highly recommend this class to those executives and managers who want to become knowledgeable about the uses and justifications of PCs in their organization. With the type of training SSE provides, PCs are sure to become a valuable tool to assist them in making informed decisions and achieving their business goals."

■ ■ ■ ■ ■

In the small business world, we focused on selected vertical markets, including law firms, advertising agencies, PR firms, job shop manufacturers, and public and independent schools. We assumed from our IBM retail referral experience that companies would acquire the software through SSE as a reseller, and then engage

SSE to implement the software. SSE grew exponentially, but we discovered that none of our revenues were coming from our targeted vertical markets. Small businesses believed the media hype about the simplicity of PCs and thought they could install them without help. They didn't understand the cost-effectiveness of what they perceived as a premium price for our services, missing out on the savings we generated by completing work successfully the first time around.

Law firm partners didn't invest in technology because expenditures came straight from their own pockets; the advertising industry was in a slump; manufacturing software vendors (such as Fourth Shift, a job shop manufacturing software) wanted to impose sales quotas on us; and educational institutions had not started budgeting for technology, such as Blackbaud software.

Along the way, we learned another valuable lesson. Blackbaud arrived in St. Louis to demonstrate its education software to Villa Duchesne, an all-girls school in St. Louis. But the trip was wasted. Blackbaud's floppy disks holding the software were wiped out when they passed through airport security. The hard lesson of backups in all forms cannot be overemphasized. It was one I learned at IBM and preach to this day.

At the end of that year, it was abundantly clear that almost all our business and the majority of our revenues were coming from large corporations. As we sought to maximize our marketing effort in time and money, we determined our small business marketing plan assumptions were erroneous. It was a harsh déjà vu of what we had learned with the Marketing Assistance Program for IBM's System 36-38 minicomputers. As a result, we ended our relationships with the software vendors and directed our efforts solely to our large corporate clients and prospects.

TAKE TIME TO BREATHE

In the midst of a grueling year, we applied a lesson in sustainability: Time out to take a breath!

Sensing that the camaraderie of our team was a key driver of our continued success, we held our first SSE Summer Outing in June 1986 for all employees at Creve Coeur Racquet Club. The idea for a "time out" to celebrate successes and build teamwork came while driving along 14th Street in downtown St. Louis with Patti Harty after a meeting at Jefferson Bank and Trust. From bemoaning

ABOVE The SSE Summer Outing, begun in 1986, remains an SSE tradition that now includes families. The first was held at Creve Coeur Racquet Club and included tennis, swimming and dinner.

the fact that everyone was on overload and picking on each other, we conceived the idea of telling the troops we were taking an afternoon off and going to "play."

In those days we played tennis (volleyball took over later), then swimming and dinner, with everyone leaving by 8 p.m. We designed our first SSE T-shirt and created a new one for this special occasion each year. Years later, the event was converted to a family occasion and locations changed as we grew, but the tradition continues unabated.

SURPRISE: MORE GROWTH HURDLES

Within just two years, we faced more infrastructure hurdles. We were pushing the limits of our 1,200-square-foot office in both staff area and training space. Our team of eight was squeezed together at desks and computers in the main space, plus demand for our training services was so strong that we needed to expand our training space from three to 10 PCs. We had discovered that 10 students was the maximum class size to ensure quality training for each student.

We moved down the street to a space that was two-and-a-half times the size of our first official office, a 3,100-square-foot office on Gardenview Office Parkway. The additional overhead was a great concern to me, and we considered subletting a room or two, but my father once again advised: "Just do it! It will be OK!" He was truly a special mentor and one of my greatest fans.

Unfortunately, my parents passed away in June of 1987 from carbon monoxide poisoning. They left a car running in the garage by mistake and never woke up the next morning. I remember that going to work was my greatest salvation since I could focus my mind on business. Several months later, however, I realized I had made commitments and decisions that I didn't recollect. The doctor whom I consulted explained to me that my forgetfulness was perfectly normal because my brain was simply on overload. There are always

BELOW Susan and her growing staff enjoyed the improved accommodations of SSE's second "real" office in 1987. The small conference room with an old dining room table grew to an office with five desks. The close quarters dictated that colleagues had to stand up and move to let others in and out of their workstation. *St. Louis Post-Dispatch* photo by Robert C. Holt, Jr., September 19, 1988.

heartbreaks in life, and I believe the lesson learned is that life must go on and that concentrated activity can actually be a salvation.

■ ■ ■ ■ ■

We decided to take our own advice in the realm of leading-edge solutions, and elected in 1987 to automate our new office with our first email system. JY selected Higgins, which was written using the first Oracle SQL database that ran on a PC network platform. Our email system only allowed sending and receiving messages among the PCs within the confines of our office. The day of emailing to destinations outside our office would wait until the Internet came along. How spoiled we are! This leading-edge implementation for SSE helped us show our prospects and clients that "we were eating our own dog food."

■ ■ ■ ■ ■

Within six months, the rapid growth of our training business brought our 10-person classroom space to 86 percent utilization, dictating the need for a second classroom. We adapted our new offices by moving furniture and walls, consuming the space I feared we might need to sublet. Theresa Ulrich Owens, our adept administrative assistant who helped grow our training business, was fond of saying, "Around here, we move furniture every three months." She was right!

Theresa was particularly dedicated. As we finalized a proposal to win the state of Missouri's training business, a torrential rainstorm knocked out our electrical power just as Theresa and I were making multiple copies of our courseware as required by the state's Request for Proposal (RFP). In the stark darkness of late evening, we blindly tried reconnecting the phone in the telephone closet to make a call out, but discovered our only direct outlet was under JY's desk. The connection was successfully made by crawling under his desk. A cell phone would have been a welcome alternative!

We met the proposal deadline of 10 a.m. the next morning and were awarded the business, but not until a full year later. Our work spanned training state workers in Word, MultiMate and IBM Reflex, a relatively unused analytical database program for the IBM PC. Unfortunately, we ended up losing a couple of our valued and very talented instructors because they didn't want to make the two-hour drive to the state capital in Jefferson City. Given that employee sentiment, we did not reapply for the contract after fulfilling our commitment of one year of training.

AND AN EARLY HURDLE OVERCOME

Having taken to heart the *INC. Magazine* adage, " ... [the] sin was not in losing a piece of business, but rather in not winning it back," we found ourselves ready in January 1988 to realize the victory of perseverance. The contract we won, our largest to date, was with Union Pacific Technologies (UPT), the same firm to which we had lost the training opportunity in 1985 when the gentleman visiting our premises found no redeeming feature in slogging over stepping-stones in the rain to reach our basement office.

UPT's objective was nationwide training on 26 IBM System 36 minicomputers at each of its railroad yards. It was an IBM referral for the training component of their installation of the S36s. After serious deliberation about the software being for midrange computers, an earlier lesson learned the hard way, we decided to take a change since it was training. We experienced a dramatic learning curve as we set up administration, travel and expense accounts, created schedules, developed the curriculum and distributed courseware by mail to each railroad yard in advance of the classes (remember no Internet yet). The revenue was a whopping $80,000!

Martha Conzelman was our lead account consultant and Bob Bock was the instructor. Because the railroad yards were thinly staffed, Bob trained half of each office (two to three people) in the morning on DisplayWrite for the IBM S36 and repeated the training for the other half in the afternoon. Sadly one day, when Bob arrived in North Platte, Nebraska, he learned the manager of the office had died that morning. UPT insisted that the show go on, however, so training proceeded as planned.

Bob saw America on SSE. He traveled to the railroad yards in his van and, instead of flying him home each weekend, we paid for his room and board as he continued his sightseeing. It was a win-win for all!

ABOVE Among SSE's key early employees were (from left) Theresa Ulrich Owens, Trent Wohlschlaeger and Martha Conzelman. © 1995 Ferguson & Katzman Photography, Inc.

CUSTOM SOLUTIONS *emerge* on PCs

Moore's Law continued its relentless expression. About every 18 months, new technology reached the market and the prices always declined. A September 20, 2010, article in the *New York Times,* "Computer as Invisible as the Air," described "the key DP/IT law" perfectly: "Moore's Law, first described in the 1960s by Douglas Engelbart and Gordon Moore, posit[ed] that computer power increases exponentially while cost falls just as quickly." For example, according to the Dataquest website, "PCs selling for less than $7,000 in 1997 will match performance of RISC-based workstations selling for $30,000 in 1996 – a two-thirds decrease" in one year.

In harmony with Moore's Law, large corporations gradually embraced the PC for cost-effective business solutions in the late 1980s and SSE's business grew. We had established solid, repeat relationships for PC-related training among St. Louis' leading companies. With our focused PC expertise and passion for solving business problems, it was natural for the training clients and word-of-mouth referrals to turn to SSE for custom applications development solutions. Our objective was to become so thoroughly integrated into each client's culture that we would win the valued status of DP partner, otherwise known as one-stop shopping!

■ ■ ■ ■ ■

Ellen Bohn, one of our first development ICs, came to us in late 1987 after the birth of her second child. Southwestern Bell (now AT&T), where she had worked for years, refused her request for a part-time schedule. Their loss was SSE's gain. Her first project was for the C.W. Freeman Gallery to manage its inventory of furniture and art items supporting its interior design practice. Today a company would buy an inventory-focused piece of software available on the open market, but the only option then was to develop a custom solution. Using R:BASE, Ellen built the application on an XT running DOS (of course) that had a 20MB hard drive, two 5.25-inch floppy disks and 256K of RAM. It took me back 27 years to the future, when my first IBM computer assignment at Monsanto was also for order entry/inventory management. This project marked the beginning of our application development (App Dev).

We designed another R:BASE system for the Emerson Electronics and Space Division. It enabled Emerson, a valued DP partner, to track its defense department bids and contracts. Ellen Bohn and Colin Havard created the application; Colin wrote the Quick Basic component.

■ ■ ■ ■ ■

Maritz Travel's business provided travel incentives to reward their clients' employees and customers. The work involved organizing and managing massive conventions for large corporations, such as automobile dealers. Because communication capabilities had not yet been developed and there was no Internet, Maritz Travel staff manually managed the administrative aspects of their events, such as room registrations, workshop schedules, sports activities sign-ups, and other aspects of group travel events. Our solution in 1988 was to download the data from Maritz Travel's headquarters mainframe in St. Louis to a PC, and then to take the PC (with appropriate backup) to the event location. This allowed daily activities, whether preregistered or not, to be managed in an automated fashion at the event site, and then uploaded to the Maritz Travel mainframe in updated form after the convention. Wow, what a concept!

■ ■ ■ ■ ■

In 1989, Bush O'Donnell & Co., Inc., founded by William H.T. "Bucky" Bush and James V. O'Donnell, acquired an Ohio company, National Elevator (NEIS). The new owners urgently needed an application to schedule, track and bill elevator inspections to replace immediately the former owner's mainframe system. Ellen Bohn and Mary Arentsen, another early SSE development IC, spent two days in Ohio to assess and define the requirements; by the time they completed their three-hour drive back to the airport, they had conceptually designed the entire system. To speed data conversion, we asked the former owner to create a magnetic tape from the mainframe, and then contracted with a St. Louis firm for the conversion from tape to floppy disks.

Our solution for NEIS was featured as the cover story in *SSE Connections,* our first newsletter, published in 1990. Illustrating the story was a photo of the World Trade Center, which NEIS inspected. With the towers destroyed on September 11, 2001, the issue is a special treasure today.

■ ■ ■ ■ ■

Parenthetically, the code generator used by Ellen on the NEIS application was redeployed by Ellen and Colin again to develop SSE's Manager System. That app was used to manage projects and feed our billing information to accounting. Susanne White, who joined SSE in November 1990, became the guru of "The

LEFT The first issue of our *SSE Connections* newsletter, published in 1990, featured SSE's work for National Elevator (NEIS) following its 1989 acquisition by Bush O'Donnell & Co. Little did anyone know that the featured World Trade Center, where NEIS provided elevator inspection services, would be destroyed 11 years later on 9/11/2001.

© Kiku Obata & Company.

Manager." She knew how to make it hum. This was a big step for us, since we had been like the "cobbler's children" and their shoes, always the last to take advantage of the latest technology. In fact, this was a good three years after JY had recognized our need and suggested Patti Harty design an order entry and billing system over a weekend.

To protect valuable "think time," we began to develop and track key business metrics:

- Acceptance ratio for Proposals in Progress (P-I-P) ran at 60 percent.
- Work In Progress (W-I-P), billed in the next quarter, tracked at 34 percent. We wondered if this could be a cash flow predictor.
- Service demand trended as reflected in our P-I-P, with about 70 percent of our proposals focused on training, 12 percent on applications development and 17 percent on consulting.

■ ■ ■ ■ ■

LEFT As SSE's business flourished we developed a robust team of professionals in application development, tech support and sales. Among them were (seated, from left) Carey Loomis (App Dev), Susan Elliott, Patti Harty (Sales), and Larry Henderson (Tech Support). Person standing was a Tech Support team member.

© 1995 Ferguson & Katzman Photography, Inc.

By 1990, we looked with pride on the representative list of clients we had been able to serve, many of them recognizable as significant in St. Louis' past and a number surviving to this day. The "Fortune Eleven," as we called them, had their world headquarters in St. Louis, and we were blessed to have all of them as clients at one time or another, delivering training, technical support and application development services.

SSE's Representative Clients in 1990

A.G. Edwards (acquired by Wells Fargo)

Angelica Uniform

Anheuser-Busch (acquired by InBev)

Bellefontaine Cemetery Association

Boatmen's Bank (acquired by Bank of America)

Brown Group

Continental Baking Co.

D'Arcy Advertising

Emerson Electric Co.

General American Life Insurance Co. (acquired by Metropolitan Life)

Internal Revenue Service (IRS)

International Shoe

Jefferson Smurfit (which became Stone Smurfit Container Corp.;
        pending acquisition by Rock-Tenn Co. in 2011)

Lutheran Church-Missouri Synod

Mallinckrodt Chemical

Maritz Travel

McDonnell Douglas (acquired by Boeing)

Mississippi River Transmission

Monsanto

Sigma-Aldrich

Southwestern Bell Corp. (acquired by AT&T)

Sverdrup (acquired by Jacobs Engineering)

Washington University Department of Surgery

WATERSHED
PERIOD
(AKA RECESSION)

After years of robust growth, the new decade presented SSE with our first challenge from outside forces: the recession of 1990-1991. The times required dramatic changes in our business model as three forces converged: our response to continued growth indicators, new federal regulations affecting technology firms and major belt-tightening among our large corporate clients. These elements shaped our next stage of growth and were instrumental in permanently changing our business model.

FOURTH OFFICE IN SEVEN YEARS

Once again our growth was felt in our work space. Colin Havard, one of our original ICs, remembered, "The developers were squeezed into the back room. If someone had to leave, everyone had to get up to let him/her get by! That room was warm except sometimes in winter, when someone would open the window, we would all freeze."

1992 RCGA ECONOMIC PROFILE ■ RESIDENTIAL CONSTRUCTION AND REAL ESTATE

MAY 1992 · ST. LOUIS · $3.00

COMMERCE

OFFICIAL PUBLICATION OF THE ST. LOUIS REGIONAL COMMERCE & GROWTH ASSOCIATION

PROBLEM SOLVER

LEFT The May 1992 edition of *St. Louis Commerce Magazine* featured Susan on the cover. Published by the St. Louis Regional Chamber & Growth Association (RCGA), the magazine often featured the business leaders serving on its board and executive committee.

Used with the permission of RCGA.

SSE's fourth office in seven years was in a more prominent location with 5,000 square feet in Creve Coeur Executive Office Park, 795 Office Parkway, close to Olive Boulevard and Interstate 270. Excessive parking space was essential to accommodate our classroom training demands, and it had to be free for our clients. Because our students came from throughout the region, we also needed a location accessible to all the major highway arteries in St. Louis.

Subsequently, we expanded our space to 7,600 square feet to accommodate more employees and a total of four classrooms. Our newly outfitted classrooms had IBM Personal System/2s (PS/2s) with 3.5-inch diskettes, which IBM introduced in an attempt to regain control of the PC market. These were configured with laser printers on a Local Area Network (LAN) to mirror our clients' sites.

INDEPENDENT CONTRACTORS BECOME EMPLOYEES

The 1986 Tax Law Act removed the Safe Harbor clause that had protected ICs and allowed firms like SSE to employ ICs rather than take on the fixed costs of employees. The ICs of many early technology companies had failed to report their incomes for tax purposes, necessitating new government rules. Section 106 of the new tax code stipulated 20 different "indicia" (requirements) to qualify for IC status. Among these, ICs had to have their own company and work for multiple organizations, as well as independently manage their work and schedule. If the preponderance of criteria were not met, the IC was presumed to be a common-law employee.

We had scheduled classes from the beginning and, as our training business grew, we wrote all of our own courseware, which our IC instructors had to use. Whether or not our ICs were registered as independent businesses, we were managing their work content and schedules. By 1990, it was clear that SSE would need to hire all our technical delivery personnel as employees. The risk and stiff penalties for noncompliance were solely on SSE.

We had not offered employee benefits to that point since we had hired people whose spouses could cover their benefits or were able to carry their own. That was no longer an option. As we planned conversion of our ICs into SSE employees, we entered the real world of health care benefits with great caution. I listened and learned from my husband, Howard, who was at Laclede Gas Co., as they were in the delicate process of downsizing their benefits.

Overnight, we grew from 23 to 47 employees, equal to about 40 Full-Time Equivalents (FTEs). We adopted a retirement plan on January 1, 1990, and then implemented the SSE Flexible Benefits Plan in late 1990. It is hard to believe, but a number of the ICs so valued their independence that they were reluctant to commit to employee status. In fact, several did not initially, but subsequently came aboard as there was no other way to work with SSE. Our business strategies and planning processes had to accommodate double the number of employees and related salary commitments and benefit costs. We had to determine how to manage productivity, and quickly learned that billability was king!

Almost minor by comparison, we purchased $100,000 of systems furniture to outfit the office. Averse to debt, we purchased with cash and were indeed fortunate to be able to draw on the nice nest egg we had built. With the same systems furniture in place 20-plus years later, however, we have experienced a great return on our investment.

In 1990, however, the combination of new technology investments, our higher fixed staff costs, increased rent and new office furniture converged at the most inopportune time.

CAUGHT IN CORPORATE BELT-TIGHTENING

These costly changes occurred just as the country headed into the recession of 1990-1991. I finally called our employees together in 1991 to explain that we would have to do some belt-tightening. Our biggest client, Monsanto, had cut back on using our services due to a surge in the cost of the raw materials derived from crude oil for its plastics business. Ellen Schmidt, one of our long-term technical employees, said, "I wondered why SSE wasn't being affected like all other companies." We limited our raises to three percent and placed some of our technical staff in positions at Monsanto at cost in order to keep the employees and stay close to a key DP partner, Monsanto. We weathered the storm without laying off anyone, befitting my IBM heritage, but we dipped into our reserves dramatically.

This was our first experience with an economic downturn. When I revived SSE in 1983, I had no clue that the country was just coming out of the serious recession of the early 1980s and that our startup timing benefitted from the improving economy in 1983 and 1984. The frugality lessons learned from 1990-1991 allowed us to avoid serious impact during the dot-com bubble burst still to come, the post-9/11 recession in 2001-2002 and the financial crisis of 2008-2009.

By the end of 1991, the demand for our services began to return. We came out of the recession faster than most traditional companies because we could provide temporary staffing for our clients so they didn't have to hire full-time employees. We experienced an incredible 66 percent growth in 1992 revenues, confirming the concept of "outsourcing." But I was silent about our success because most other companies were still struggling, and I was reluctant to admit that our business was soaring. We were fortunate in our timing, as we were in 1983 and so often throughout the years.

■ ■ ■ ■ ■

Our SSE Advisory Board was there for us through thick and thin as we steered our course through the dramatic business learning curve. We continued to refine and review with them our marketing goals and objectives with our continued theme, "Build Relationships." The meetings shifted to be much more focused on how we do business, how to deal with markets and processes to bring in business, as well as how to address economic situations. We had outgrown our startup issues with our new business model and were now shifting to sustain business on firm ground. This was a natural evolution and surely a good sign!

GOING
NATIONAL

The continuing evolution and interaction of hardware, software and networking just before our 10th anniversary in 1993 kindled our growth well beyond a "St. Louis company" to become a national player.

A series of technical advancements set the stage for greater collaboration on the national stage as DP (Data Processing) shifted to IT (Information Technology):

- The first search engine, dubbed Archie, was created in 1990 by Alan Emtage, a student at McGill University in Montreal.
- On August 6, 1991, the World Wide Web (www) project made its debut as a publicly available service on the Internet.
- In 1991, Microsoft released the first version of Visual Basic. That gave the masses the power to develop graphical Windows applications through a very easy-to-use WYSIWYG (What You See Is What You Get) design process, paired with the BASIC programming language.

- By 1992, client/server technology was recognized and competitive, with Oracle, Sybase and SQL emerging as early leaders.
- SSE's typical class offerings then were Lotus Notes, as we became a Lotus Notes Valued-Added Reseller (VAR) and Business Partner, plus OS/2 2.0, Microsoft NT, Windows for Workgroups, Access and Visual Basic.

Technology Platforms of 1990

- Hardware platforms:
  - Micros aka PCs
  - IBM AS/400
  - DEC VAX
  - Novell LANs
  - Apple Macintosh
- Operating systems:
  - Micros: MS/DOS, OS/2, Unix/Xenix
  - LANs: Novell, 3COM-Ethernet, IBM PC LAN
- Software:
  - Word Processors: WordPerfect
  - Spreadsheets: Lotus, QuattroPro, Excel
  - Application Development: dBASE, FoxPro, Paradox, R:BASE, Quick Basic, C
  - Accounting: SBT

■ ■ ■ ■ ■

Training remained a dominant force in the PC world in the early 1990s as companies sought to keep up with the advantages IT promised to deliver. The latest technology explosion drove the need for training nationwide. Our large corporate clients needed to standardize their training and provide a consistent message at all branches and plants.

Others were recognizing the same market demand, including Logical Operations, Inc., a training firm in Rochester, New York, that later sold to Ziff Communications Co. in 1991. Inspired by its client, Kodak, Logical Operations proposed to build a consortium of training companies. Called the National Training Matrix, the consortium sought to provide accessibility to training across the country. The curriculum was to consist of Windows, Lotus 1-2-3, Excel, dBASE, WordPerfect, Microsoft Word and Microsoft Word for Windows. A number of other firms expressed interest in national training solutions, including NCR, Xerox, 3M, Mobil and Sears.

Our training director, Stu Cassista, and I flew to Rochester to meet the Matrix partners. Elements of the program included a toll-free registration number and a "Learn or Return" guarantee to make the solution attractive, plus free coffee. We joined the Matrix, but its life span was short. The training companies in the consortium were just independent enough that it was hard to make the concept work effectively. Yet it highlighted the need among large multioffice corporations for solutions that delivered consistent training nationwide.

■ ■ ■ ■

Concurrently, we knew we had to reform our training practice internally. We learned the hard way that when corporations cut costs, training is often first on the chopping block. Clients' efforts to cut training costs drove huge price pressures from large corporations as they continued downsizing. We accepted volume strategies rather than lose a client, but quickly learned that the volume discount imposed by Anheuser-Busch was counterproductive. With every new staffing position or engagement, the more money we lost!

But there was a payoff. Retaining the relationship with Anheuser-Busch gave us a chance to win the training development and delivery for its customized processes for using SAP, a comprehensive business management software system that was new to the market. Anheuser-Busch contracted to send our instructors to deliver the training at all its U.S. plants. Training was delivered at their convenience, of course, which even included training on the third shift. This proved to be a profitable initiative!

Since decreased corporate training demands coincided with doubling our overhead as ICs became employees, we sought to fill the financial gap by offering more public classes. It was "back to the future," a throwback to our HI-U classes at the Ladue School District during our early years, when we had to concern ourselves with maintaining profitability based on revenue per student. It had become far easier and more profitable to sell out an entire class, or even multiple classes, to a single client than it was to sell to individuals. We trusted that the enlarged footprint of our marketplace exposure was a great lead generator for marketing our other services. It was important to get it right.

We formed a Training Task Force, led by Charlie Young, another former IBMer. We charged it with determining our training focus going forward and recommending directions and tactics for profitable operations and growth. At one point, as the analysis and discussion of our training business evolved, our Advisory Board recommended that we get out of the training business altogether. Thank heaven we resisted, paving the way for our longest and richest heritage. Our Blended Learning/eLearning services have remained a primary, award-winning strength. With our mantra, "nothing as constant as change," eLearning morphed into mLearning (mobile Learning) in 2010.

FIRST TRY AT GROWTH BY ACQUISITION

Our growing national exposure through clients and such initiatives as the National Training Matrix consortium began to yield acquisition opportunities, as both buyer and seller. National TechTeam in Detroit was among those interested in partnering with or acquiring SSE, but nothing worthwhile materialized. Productivity Point, a global training network, invited SSE to join its group, but we would have lost too much autonomy, so we declined.

In St. Louis, we entered into discussions in late 1992 to acquire Productivity Plus, one of our competitors. Ultimately, after completing negotiations and spending $80,000 in legal fees, the merger talks broke down the night before sealing the deal. My negative response to being asked if we also would buy one of the principal's home PCs was apparently the straw that broke the deal. In hindsight, the difficulty of the decision to sell was understandable, and I believe the owners simply were not ready.

The good news was that the seeds of the relationship grew some roots and we did finally merge in 1998, a new application of the adage, " … [the] sin was not in losing, but rather in not winning it back." Loire Kroeger and Eileen Weber joined SSE and we were indeed fortunate to have them, their clients and their expertise on our team.

DISTANCE LEARNING

NCR/AT&T invited SSE in 1993 to its world headquarters in Dayton, Ohio, to view its extensive education satellite and multimedia capabilities. Patti Harty, our newly named Manager of Sales and Marketing; Lisa Olenski, our new Manager of Education Services; JY and I drove to Dayton because that was the only way we could afford to get all four of us there. Our goal was twofold: see their distance-learning capabilities and create a partnership. One of the gentlemen we met taught me the phrase that I have enjoyed using ever since: "The answer is yes! What is the question?"

NCR/AT&T's initial distance-learning solution to Computer-Based Training (CBT) was a satellite-based system. The uplink at NCR headquarters was the expensive component. The PCs on which the students could attend the training functioned as the downlinks. A live instructor was at the uplink, and all the students transmitted questions through the satellite system to the instructor's PC.

The trip resulted in the SSE-NCR/AT&T agreement, announced in December 1993, to jointly market education services to Fortune 500 customers. The partnership provided SSE clients with consistent training on a nationwide basis, either in a classroom setting or using CBT, multimedia and the satellite uplink. We even gained the privilege of using the NCR/AT&T logo on our marketing materials. This was just the solution we needed to address the training needs of large corporate clients, a huge advance over the classroom-only concept proposed only three years earlier with the National Training Matrix. Internet training was not an option yet, as there was not enough bandwidth for courseware to be delivered over the web. It would be another nine years before technological advancements would give us the opportunity to deploy web-based training solutions worldwide.

The SSE-NCR/AT&T agreement was a perfect example of the staggering speed of change in the IT industry. Business needs and entrepreneurial drive were advancing technology, and the leading-edge technology was facilitating our advances in service offerings to solve our clients' evolving needs. This sustained the cycle with which we had grown familiar. Companies were willing to pay for assistance with new technology and leading-edge solutions, but ultimately took work in-house when sufficient internal knowledge was developed to do so cost-effectively. This was true for both training and PC support.

10 years STRONG

In the same 1991-1993 time span, our billings were focused on PC support at Monsanto and Southwestern Bell (SBC). We billed more than 12,000 hours of tech support to Monsanto alone in one year. We developed such an effective working relationship with them that when they asked us to hire in advance of their needs, we obliged.

"ONE-UP" TECH SUPPORT

The approach, which we called our "one-up" strategy, ensured we had the technical support personnel oriented and ready when Monsanto called. It was a win-win approach for both of us until Monsanto spun off its chemical company as the newly formed Solutia at the end of the century and decided to outsource all of its IT support to IBM.

In a Goliath beats David move, IBM immediately hired all 25 PC support people away from SSE, a sizable financial hit. Monsanto had worried for several years that they were responsible for more than 30 percent of our income, so this rapidly solved that problem for them. Larry Henderson, head of SSE's PC Support and another former IBMer, did a great job of managing us through that situation. Solutia also outsourced its IT to Electronic Data Systems (EDS), which caused a few more losses for us.

Today we wouldn't dream of hiring "one-up" to the "bench" just in case we would get a request. Not only would it destroy our profitability, but staffing demands among our individual clients have grown too diverse for this approach to be workable.

APP DEV EVOLVES

The corporate world was just beginning to recognize and trust that it could put mission-critical applications (apps) on PCs. No significant broad-based transition occurred, however, until we had client/server technology, coincident with our 10-year anniversary in 1993. Some of the leading-edge applications that swiftly followed reinforced the PC's power and trustworthiness.

From 1991 to 1993, Ellen Bohn developed a series of applications using Clipper Summer '87 for Monsanto and Maverick Tube. Mike Jones, another one of our developers, had written a library of routines for Clipper that greatly simplified the development of the DOS apps.

We also developed a system to track the bar codes for Chirometrics' chiropractic practice in Effingham, Illinois. This was our first experience at "virtual development" since there was still no Internet. We were a long way from home, but we completed it successfully and our work was featured as the cover story in one of our newsletters. This project was truly heaven-sent, as it was among the first App Dev projects we won coming out of the recession.

In August 1993, we began helping our corporate clients "right-size" their mainframe systems with client/server applications. To develop these Windows apps accompanied by a database with a much richer user interface, we made major changes in our SSE toolset. By the mid-1990s, we had switched from Clipper to Access and Visual Basic for the Graphical User Interface (GUI) front ends, and we were developing the server databases using PowerBuilder and C++.

Not surprisingly, our first such app was for Monsanto to track and forecast product distribution data stored on multiple mainframes. In addition, Ellen Bohn developed Access apps for Maritz, Magna Bank and Payne Electric (now PayneCrest Electric & Communications), for whom Ellen has provided development services continuously for almost two decades. We continued to benefit from our commitment to delivering the highest quality services and exceeding our clients' expectations, proving once again that building long-term relationships through trustworthy service and value generates project after project, year after year.

STRATEGY FOR ACCELERATION

At 10 years of age, the PC industry was maturing and so was SSE. The post-recession period served as a springboard to SSE's next stage of growth by every measure: business activity, revenue, costs and employees. Revenues were up by 40 to 50 percent over the prior year in the first half of the fiscal year ending February 28, 1993. We were intent on remembering the lessons we learned during the recession: stay lean, keep the organization flat (such as eliminating the secretarial function) and keep expenses variable. To do so, we returned to our original IC model in a new form, using "associate" or part-time hourly employees, especially for instructors who welcomed the flexibility.

Our drive for flexibility matched the needs of our large corporate clients. They continued to favor using temporary help until they gained solid earnings growth and felt safe bringing "the temps" on as full-time employees. The wave of productivity gains attributable to technology was reflected in reduced hiring overall. Each person aided by technology could accomplish far more work than in pre-PC days. The same phenomenon of fewer people doing more work occurred again after the dot-com bubble burst in 2001-2002 and the financial crisis of 2008-2009.

Our fast pace of growth necessitated hiring nearly 30 employees in about one year, bringing our total employment to more than 60 people. We managed that personnel growth with the development of job descriptions, processes and tools for supporting career expectations and benefit demands. Competition had become keener as others recognized our market had merit. The PC industry had come of age, from startup to thriving, in just 10 years. We had to learn to articulate and demonstrate what distinguished SSE, what value-add we produced and what was unique about us. One of my favorite themes for managing business growth was "Minding Your Ps and a Q: Price, Productivity, Pipeline, (Work-in-) Progress, Project Management and People mean Profitability and Quality."

Another outgrowth of industry maturation and the emergence of App Dev was recurring acquisition activity. One organization that approached SSE about partnering or merging was Earl Lindenberg & Associates, a mainframe and minicomputer shop, also based in St. Louis. We ultimately determined that combination could not be successful because they didn't understand our PC business. A number of other acquisitions were considered, but the circumstances were never quite right, affirming time and again that it is tough to find a good fit.

CULTURE CULTIVATION

Recognizing that our employees were as important to our success as our clients, we conceived the idea to recognize their commitment and contributions with the creation of the Five Years and More Club. We wanted to celebrate employees who were with us for the "long period" of five years and recognize their commitment to stellar client service. The club has met annually ever since for lunch in the fall, at which time the new five-year employees are initiated with a plaque for their offices and a watch with the SSE logo on its face. Each year, we distribute stickers to be affixed to update the plaques to indicate the additional year of service. An oversized plaque in our lobby adds each person's name in sequence by the year he/she was initiated.

Sitting around the table at lunch in order of tenure, with the oldest on my right and the newest on my left, our conversations always generated a trip down memory lane as we reminisced at length. Without recognizing it at the time, I was solidifying our culture with SSE team members most likely to continue cultivating it into the future. I would start the discussion with a question, such as "What do you remember most about starting with SSE?" or "What technology was in vogue?" Then each person around the table would respond, inspiring other

---

BELOW SSE's 10th anniversary in 1993 was celebrated with the firm's 70 employees and their families at the St. Louis Science Center.

recollections. One of my favorite questions was: "Where were you in 1966 when I founded SSE?" Many of them had not yet been born!

This special SSE tradition continues today and is one of my favorites!

■ ■ ■ ■

Our first 10 years of service culminated at the end of 1993 with a big bash at the St. Louis Science Center for our employees and their spouses. It was an ideal opportunity to express thanks to all of those who created and nurtured our success, even though one among them called me a "tough old bird!"

THE RAPID PACE OF TECHNOLOGY CHANGE

Our *SSE Connections* newsletter commemorated our 10th anniversary year with a comparison between 1983 and 1993, chronicling the rapid pace of change in technology. Note in "Most Important Words to Define," the Internet jargon did not yet appear.

	1983	1993
Office Location	400 sq ft in basement	Three offices later—7,600 sq ft in modern office park
Number of Employees	1	70
Number of Clients	1	Hundreds
Training Facility	Ladue School District "pods"	SSE offices—four classrooms
PC Configuration	64K RAM One 360K diskette drive Monochrome monitor 4.77MHz 8088 processor $4,200	8MB RAM 250MB hard drive Super VGA color monitor 33MHz 486 processor $2,000
PC Vendors	IBM, Apple	IBM, Compaq, Apple and a host of "house brands"
Favorite Word Processor	WordStar with DisplayWrite not far behind	WordPerfect for DOS Word for Windows
Favorite Spreadsheet	VISICALC (Lotus 1-2-3 was just beginning to advertise)	Lotus 1-2-3 in DOS Excel in Windows
Favorite Database	dBASE II	Clipper & FoxPro for developers; Paradox for end-users
Most Important Words to Define	Hardware, software, floppy disk (there were no hard drives yet), DOS	Client/server, object-oriented programming, SQL, LAN and WAN, interoperability, API

SECOND DECADE
of LEADING-EDGE
SOLUTIONS

With a great and capable team of 70, hundreds of loyal clients and the strength of continuous innovation, our growth continued unabated. We expanded across the hall in the Creve Coeur Executive Office Park, occupying a total of almost 10,000 square feet. A new addition to our desktops was the "mouse pad," introduced in 1993!

As we headed into our second decade, the President's Message in the Summer 1994 *SSE Connections* newsletter described our thrilling ride: "How many of us have ridden in a Model-T? Perhaps in a reproduction but ... not many in the real thing. What if I were to suggest that today you are bumping down a rutted dirt road in the equivalent?"

The message went on to say that SSE had a unique historical perspective on the automation process. We were one of the first in St. Louis to:

- Design and deliver training for end users
- Pioneer the PC support function

- Adapt a structured methodology to PC application development in order to quality-assure our services
- Rank as the only information services firm focused exclusively on the delivery of integrated solutions at the desktop

The message continued: " ... linking telecommunications and computer technology for shared data and resources make it possible – and necessary – to have information instantly available for the decision-maker ... Not only do more people have PCs on their desks, but twice as much work is being done by fewer people. People are working at home and people are working in teams with the need to connect worldwide ... As businesses continue to access and utilize information to communicate and compete globally – and as the information highway becomes reality – I submit that we will flash back to the last decade of the twentieth century and see a picture of the information age Model-T." What a prophetic statement!

In 1994, SSE launched the next generation of our support services: a subscription service for PC users (not corporations) named PC+911. We considered a number of options for "going retail" with our approach to harvest and serve available customers, just as we had in the early years in supporting the first IBM PC buyers. Our first strategy was to seek a partnership with Wal-Mart to offer on-site technology support in each store's vestibule, "next door" to businesses offering eyeglasses, clinics and the like. The concept anticipated that people would carry in their PCs to have them fixed while they were shopping.

LEFT SSE developed a subscription service for PC users branded as PC+911 in 1994, which became SSE+911. The service rollout coincided with experiments by SSE to take its services to retail settings. © Kiku Obata & Company.

Kiku Obata, Founder and CEO of Kiku Obata & Company, who had designed our *SSE Connections* newsletters, stepped up again to design a layout for a vestibule service center. We worked with Jack Moore, the Wal-Mart executive in charge of its vestibule leasing program, and they were very interested, but we would have had to rent the "real estate" for each facility. That was the "showstopper!"

The Wal-Mart vestibule services were fashioned as a "sit and wait" business model versus our "develop and serve" approach to delivering expertise to corporate clients, and one in which we would have been out on the fringe again. With wonderful 20/20 hindsight, we were lucky Wal-Mart made it too expensive and difficult for us to risk what surely would have been short-lived at best. The pace of change in technology would have put us in a position of massive real estate obligations as the retail service model grew obsolete. While always analyzing and taking risks rather than maintaining status quo and sliding backwards, choosing which innovations to implement was just as critical as which ones to reject. It reinforced our important lesson learned on focus!

■ ■ ■ ■ ■

Next we conceived the idea of developing a partnership with Computer City (sold to CompUSA in 1998 and liquidated) to piggyback the sale of our services onto customers buying PCs in its stores. Charlie Young and I traveled to Computer City's headquarters in Fort Worth, Texas, to sell the idea in 1994. We received the go-ahead to place our brochures and offer our service as a pilot in the St. Louis store in Bridgeton and one in Miami, Florida. We had a customer from Miami so impressed with the service that he wanted to sell it over his cable TV network, and a Miami physician volunteered to serve as a PC+911 reference. Despite the few successes, a big push and good press, the program did not take off. The salespeople in the store were "techies" who loved to help their customers themselves. Besides, their assistance came free, a price against which we obviously could not compete. It took me back 20 years to when the Famous-Barr computer salesman was the "trainer" for my first PC.

Ultimately, our PC+911 service product was questioned from a trademark standpoint, so we changed it to SSE+911, which was more beneficial to SSE branding anyway. At the time, we were registering an average of 150 to 200 calls per day, and finally we could add Internet support! The Internet was now accessible, though mostly by slow dial-up connections. We were busy implementing solutions that used the much-awaited capability.

One key SSE + 911 client was Peabody Coal, whose mines in Wyoming needed after-hours tech support. We expanded our help desk service to 24/7 (24 hours a day, seven days a week) to take a handoff from them at 5 p.m. and then turned control back to Peabody's help desk in the early morning. We were able to staff the support desk with interns from Webster University and the University of Missouri–St. Louis, none of whom minded being up all night or working on the weekends. These young people worked for $10 an hour and loved it because it was an opportunity to earn decent money and provide a service of real value. As client demand lapsed, SSE's help desk support function went dormant until our introduction of Pretecht in 2005.

■ ■ ■ ■ ■

Our technical support services were evolving with the creation of a new business unit, "Placement Offsite," eventually known as Staff Augmentation. Monsanto and other large corporate clients needed full-time technical support in-house, but still preferred to outsource rather than hire full-time employees with benefits. The arrangement was a stable cash generator for SSE, since our associates were employed on an hourly basis, so every hour of a 40-hour (or more) week at the client site was billable. Subsequently, when corporate earnings were sustainably strong, the corporations would hire the "temps" as employees since it was more cost-effective, even with benefits.

This service approach was based on an entirely different business model that required 24-hour response by the vendor; the client choice was based on lowest cost, not necessarily quality; and a full complement of skill sets was needed rather than just our PC expertise. While it seemed like a good fit at the time, it failed to align with our best service delivery practices in succeeding years and was spun off from SSE in 2009. This became another focus lesson learned.

NETWORK SERVICES & INTEGRITY

Our network practice was evolving, replacing the days of "sneaker net" when the only way people "networked" was to hand-carry 5.25-inch and then 3.5-inch diskettes from one PC to the next. We introduced our first technical support contract, Peak Performance Agreement, to provide monthly computer and network support for small businesses.

An incident occurred in those early network days that gave us a message to deliver and redeliver on the importance of impeccable integrity as expressed by each employee and the company as a whole. A new company sought our help on a Windows NT network. We had not had much experience with the new network, so were reluctant to take the business. The client begged us to just make a trip to his office and said he had $100,000 to invest with us if we could help. With many caveats, we went to his office and discovered, to our dismay, that he was building a pornographic bulletin board. Our network engineer was shocked, but worried about alerting SSE because he didn't want us to lose the $100,000, a huge sum in those days. Thankfully, he did.

I called our attorney to ensure we would not be caught in a legal snare and then contacted the gentleman to decline any further business. We never billed him. This incident inspired me to deliver a clear and unequivocal message to all of our employees serving clients at their sites, seeing and hearing things we would not know, that all of SSE was there to back them up. Time and again, our message to our team was, and is, that SSE's integrity and each person's own integrity are more important than anything else, without compromise.

Subsequently, we had another network incident that allowed me to deliver the same message of impeccable integrity. It arose after a new law tied to the emerging network services business required a company with multiple workstations to buy a license for each device. We were asked to implement a small network, but this client insisted on buying one software license only. We installed his one license on one PC, and the next week he proceeded to try copying the software to his other PCs. When that didn't work, he called us again. We explained that he would have to buy the additional licenses because he was violating the law, and he replied, "Well, if I had known you were that type of company, I wouldn't have engaged you." Clearly we did no further business with him, nor did we bill his company for our services. By observing these actions, our uncompromising attitude toward integrity was reinforced for our engineers in the field.

Clearly we had numerous outstanding experiences in 1993, including our work with MICDS, the merged institution of Mary Institute and St. Louis Country Day School. We were engaged to network the campus, including capabilities for multimedia and Internet video, email, file sharing, classroom use, and the traditional business and administration management applications.

INTERNET SERVICES EMERGE

The first graphical web browser, Mosaic, was released in 1993. Mosaic fired up an explosion in web use and the transition to Internet connectivity in our homes and workplaces. Mosaic was the forerunner to Netscape, introduced by Marc Andreessen in 1994, which garnered 90 percent of all web usage at its peak. Then Microsoft's Internet Explorer (IE) came to market in 1995, initiating the industry's first browser war. By bundling with Windows, Microsoft's IE was able to leverage its dominance to take over the web browser market, generating IE usage share that exceeded 95 percent by 2002 (later declining to 60 percent browser usage share by September 2010).

SSE developed a leading-edge application with Mosaic for McDonnell Douglas Corp. (MDC) in 1994. When MDC had a plane crash, which they called an "incident," the ensuing investigation required lugging all their manuals to the incident site to document each piece of evidence in minute detail. We designed an application that allowed them to scan the heavy volumes of data in their manuals into a database on a PC. They could then travel to the incident site carrying only the PC. They used Mosaic to retrieve the key details from the database and notate the pertinent incident information directly on the PC. Mosaic was free, open-source software, a new concept for all of us!

Internet strategies began to be contemplated not only by our clients, but also by the "cobbler's children." In 1995, we launched our first website with the foresight and help of one of our key developers, Jeff Barczewski. Since "SSE" was taken as a domain name, we settled for SSEinc, as in www.SSEinc.com.

ABOVE SSE's first website was launched in 1995 with the domain name of www.SSEinc.com.

■ ■ ■ ■ ■

A series of Internet-based advancements quickly ensued:

- Jeff Bezos went online with Amazon.com in 1996.

- Iranian computer programmer, Pierre Omidyar, also went online in 1996 with a personal auction website called AuctionWeb. The very first auction was for a broken laser pointer, which sold for $14.83. After contacting the winning bidder to verify that he/she was aware the laser pointer was broken, the winner responded, "I collect broken laser pointers." By 1997, AuctionWeb had officially changed its name to eBay, and still sells broken laser pointers.

- Sun Microsystems (bought by Oracle in early 2010) released at this same time the first version of the Java language with its Netscape browser platform.

- Intranets were being implemented to harness the power of the Internet within companies. For instance, the Federal Reserve Bank extensively used an intranet to disseminate published information, thereby eliminating manual printing costs and time barriers (according to Killen & Associates in 1996).

COMPUTER-BASED TRAINING ARRIVES

It wasn't long before SSE started training on the Internet. The web-based training was truly a déjà vu experience. Here we were again, forging into new territory, defining a new technology and new terms, such as ".com," "domain name" and "World Wide Web" or www. Our first such project in 1995, teaching proper Internet procedures and etiquette for Blue Cross Blue Shield in St. Louis, was also noteworthy as our first actual delivery of computer-based training. Actual web-based or training delivered over the Internet was still another seven years away.

In addition to the new Internet training, the launch of Windows 95 and the Microsoft Office Suite, consisting of Word, Excel and PowerPoint, generated a great burst of new training. SSE maintained its lead position as the trainer of choice among St. Louis-based corporations looking to speed new software adoption in their organizations. Within four days of its August 24, 1995 release, Microsoft sold more than a million copies of Microsoft Windows 95.

To enhance our public classroom training offerings, our Q2 (second quarter) 1995 PC Training Class Schedule announced that SSE would award 0.6 of a Continuing Education Unit (CEU) to each student who successfully completed a day of training. By meeting the standards for earning nationally recognized

LEFT SSE promoted a wide array of training classes for public enrollment through a quarterly publication after newspaper advertising proved fruitless. By the second quarter of 1995, SSE awarded a 0.6 Continuing Education Unit (CEU) for each completed class. © Kiku Obata & Company.

credit for training programs, we found a new way to differentiate the quality of our training against competitors. To ensure an "official" look to each CEU certificate, we embossed each with our corporate seal and practically wore it out. The imprint from our original corporate seal is faint today.

Brenda Enders, now SSE's Chief Learning Strategist & Practice Leader for Learning Services, was still in our instructor-led training mode. For many students, she remembers, this was the first time they used a mouse. It was fairly common for students to pick up the mouse and move it in the air, thinking that would move the arrow on the screen. Several times, she said, "We had students trying to use the wall as their mouse pads." Others were afraid to pick up the mouse at all.

■ ■ ■ ■ ■

A special "one-off" story was an opportunity to train a friend, Bill Culver, suffering with ALS or "Lou Gehrig's Disease," on how to use a PC so he could communicate with those around him. The software was created for Stephen Hawking, a British theoretical physicist and cosmologist, who was almost completely paralyzed from ALS. Keystrokes were coded to reflect different messages, so Bill could depress one key and a message would be printed. Ultimately, flicks of the eye were able to generate printed messages. As this was not mainstream for SSE, we asked one of our instructors, Bette Schlie, to learn how to use the system and then she regularly went to Bill's house to assist him.

Like other SSE team members before her, Bette joined SSE by an unusual path. I had met her husband in conversation on an airplane and he said they were moving back to St. Louis. I gave him my business card and Bette called when they arrived. I hired her, and she played a lead role as both an instructor and as a technical support team member for a number of years.

APP DEV SERVICES EXPAND

Ellen Bohn, consistently first with our leading-edge solutions, remembers her first Windows application experience. She discussed a new project with a prospective client and suggested writing the application in the new Windows software. The client was adamant that he didn't want a Windows app; he wanted a DOS app. Even after discussing the advantages of a Windows app, he refused to change his mind. When asked to explain, he said he feared his employees would spend too much time playing solitaire with Windows running on their PCs. Ultimately the system was developed as a Windows app.

Ellen continued her many firsts by developing a series of applications for RehabCare using Visual FoxPro. Visual FoxPro, a more robust programming language than Access, provided a rich Windows user interface along with a powerful database engine. These apps ran on individual PCs, each having its own copy of the data, as the DP/IT world had not evolved yet to the concept of data stored on a centralized server. Some of these apps are still in use. A number of clients continued to rely on SSE for new app development, and RehabCare returned in 2010, but this time, for a mobile learning solution.

In 1995, Graybar Electric's objective was to provide its customers worldwide with the capability to initiate orders online in their native time zone. What a novel idea! Graybar gave each customer a PC with the software loaded on it. What made it even more leading-edge technically was that Graybar still had an old Honeywell mainframe system at its headquarters in St. Louis. Carey Loomis, SSE's lead developer on the project, had to parse the messages coming from customers' PCs so Graybar's mainframe could accept them in an understandable format. It was quite a feat!

In addition, SSE built our first version control system with the application, which meant we would "push out" software updates simultaneously to all the PCs so every customer was on the same version of the application at all times. This was another new concept.

Bridge Information Systems engaged SSE to develop a Sequel (SQL) Server application to access and coordinate the complex agreements between financial service clients and the various international exchanges. An even bigger Bridge commitment came several years later, a perfect example of the importance of building relationships to gain repeat business. It helped, of course, to have Terry Franc, one of the founders of Bridge, on our Advisory Board, as that exposure gave him knowledge and confidence in our capabilities for mission-critical work.

WBE ACHIEVEMENT

Despite widespread recognition of our company in the technology world, it was 1998 before SSE achieved Women's Business Enterprise (WBE) certification by the national organization, Women's Business Enterprise National Council

(WBENC) in partnership with the Women's Business Development Center in Chicago. This was a long-fought battle by many women business owners. A woman who founded a business was presumed to be a fraud and a shill for some male until she could prove it otherwise. We dubbed this "being guilty until proven innocent."

In applying for WBE certification with the state of Missouri, after all the documentation was completed and an on-site visit had occurred (where my husband was nowhere to be found), the state pronounced that SSE could not possibly be a woman-owned business because my SSE stock was in my revocable trust and my husband was the beneficiary of the trust! After contacting people we knew in the Governor's office, they sheepishly allowed an exception to permit SSE to be certified. Within a year, the outdated regulation was rescinded.

Monsanto requested that we seek the WBE certification so they could demonstrate and receive credit for the use of small businesses and minorities. IBM was pleased to use the certification when Monsanto outsourced its tech support to them. Later, it was helpful in seeking an entrée into government business, but it was never the blockbuster that it was proclaimed to be.

KEY INTERNAL ACQUISITION

Capping off the exciting year of 1995, my daughter, Elizabeth, joined SSE in the fall. In the four years following her 1991 graduation from the University of Vermont, Elizabeth worked for Esprit in San Francisco, a wholesaler of kids' and teens' clothes. She began on staff in Esprit's Outlet Store and then progressed through the ranks to assist in rolling out a new line of products under the coveted Dr. Seuss logo. All of her experiences at Esprit provided her with a virtual MBA through on-the-job training ("MBA-OJT").

It was clear to me that she had a good business head on her shoulders and was an especially good decision-maker. We tried once unsuccessfully in the spring of 1995 to lure her back to St. Louis and into SSE, but Esprit "hung the moon" to keep her. We tried again that fall when we had an opening for a sales account executive, and explained that we could only offer her a position when there was one available. Actually, Howard and I were on a trip around the world on the Concorde celebrating his retirement from Laclede Gas, and in that three-week period Elizabeth gave two weeks' notice and worked a week at SSE before we returned. We were thrilled that she made the big leap!

For the first year, she always introduced herself as Elizabeth, never using her last name. We barely spoke in the office because she was intent on establishing her own identity. She also never directly reported to me, which was important in the transition.

Subsequently, she ran our Solutions Division, responsible for delivering our infrastructure and custom software development services. Then in 2001, she became Vice President of Business Development, and ultimately President in 2004. I like to think this, too, was a leading-edge solution in succession planning from mother to daughter. We were and are blessed to have her!

EXCELLENCE REWARDED

Recognizing that a company's assets go "down the elevator" and home every night, we realized it was critical for us to enable their highest level of success and acknowledge how they made the exceptional difference. Max De Pree, CEO of Herman Miller, Inc., wrote a book in 1987, *Leadership is an Art,* that articulated this concept.

Just as we had reinforced the importance of longevity among our employees with SSE's Five Years and More Club, we decided to recognize individual contributions to our success with establishment of the SSE Achievement of Excellence Award:

"The SSE Achievement of Excellence Award is given to an SSE employee who has attained a level of distinction in his/her field that clearly differentiates the individual and SSE in the Information Technology industry. This individual employee's achievements contribute significantly toward fulfilling SSE's vision of technical excellence and superior service."

The first recipients in 1996 were Korky Holton, Sales; Mark Kloth and Ed Ulkus, Networks; and Madhuri Gururaj, Barry Marcus and Trent Wohlschlaeger, Application Development. Almost every year since then, at least one SSE employee has been acknowledged for his or her unique contributions.

■ ■ ■ ■ ■

In the category of keeping our employees happy, as well as protecting our recruitment and retention success, SSE had to consider the possibility of Casual Fridays, unthinkable from my old IBM days.

Under Elizabeth's leadership, blue jeans became *de rigueur.* One delightful anecdote: my husband and I were traveling out of the country and were delayed leaving Kennedy Airport in New York. In the waiting lounge, a huge new device accepted credit cards for Internet access. I was excited to dial up my SSE mailbox and there I discovered a message to all: "Mom's gone. You can wear blue jeans tomorrow." I busted her message that evening, and they still all wore blue jeans the next day. They simply left me out of the loop for any future pranks!

SEA CHANGE *period*

In 1998, SSE became Novell's first and only Platinum Partner in St. Louis, just as we were simultaneously establishing a closer working relationship with Microsoft. Novell had about 70 percent of the market, which they inevitably lost to Microsoft. A favorite memory involved Jeff Raikes, the seventh employee at Microsoft, who always stopped at the Microsoft regional office in St. Louis on his way to visit his parents in Nebraska. As a Microsoft Partner, he asked for a special meeting with me to determine how important our Novell relationship was and to encourage us to jump exclusively onto the Microsoft NT bandwagon.

Jeff and I met in an office so tiny that our knees were practically touching to discuss ending our Novell relationship so that Microsoft could feel comfortable sending us a ton of business. First I observed that Microsoft was a product-centric business, whereas SSE was focused on solving business problems with a purely client-focused, client-driven approach.

Then I explained we had to be in charge of our own destiny and be responsible for developing our own business. We had determined in the late 1980s that we couldn't depend on IBM to bring us business through the Marketing Assistance Program since the IBM sales reps were not our clients, but thought they were. Most of the companies of our ilk that relied solely on IBM and subsequently on Microsoft eventually went out of business. Another lesson learned, and reinforced!

Novell, with about 70 percent market share, was a major source of revenue for us. We simply could not turn our backs on it. Furthermore, from an integrity standpoint, I could not get a lead from Novell and convert it to a Microsoft opportunity, just as I couldn't condone clones years earlier when IBM had given us PC leads. I did commit, however, to recommend Microsoft when it was the most appropriate network solution for our client and there were no strings attached. Jeff said that was fine "as clearly it would function under the Trojan horse theory."

When Jeff retired from Microsoft in July 2008 to join Microsoft Founder Bill Gates in his charitable foundation, I emailed a congratulatory note to him. He, too, remembered our meeting and conversation from 10 years earlier.

A year or so later, we decided to drop Novell and focus 100 percent of our network services attention on Microsoft because our association with Novell continued to be a detriment to getting Microsoft leads. As I recall, this was a decision Elizabeth made when she led our Solutions Division. Vince Sechrest, now SSE's Network Services Practice Leader, remembered one of the drivers of this decision was that we were unable to get support from Novell to resolve a bug in the GroupWise mail system we had deployed at Missouri State Bank. If we could not get Novell support as a Platinum Partner, then we felt we were much better off with Microsoft. Unfortunately, we had to refer Missouri State Bank to another company, and that was so very difficult because the bank had been a great client.

Shortly thereafter, we became a Microsoft Gold Partner and remain so to this day. As a testament to our relationship, we partnered with Microsoft to highlight the release of Windows 2000 with our second event at the St. Louis Science Center. We demonstrated Windows 2000 on the Omnimax screen to our clients and it was a huge (no pun intended) hit. As part of the celebration, Vince Sechrest and Kevin Grossnicklaus collaborated on a game, "Who wants

ABOVE F. Mark Kuhlmann (right), former Senior Vice President and General Counsel of McDonnell Douglas, joined Susan in leading SSE as President in 1998.

to go to Windows 2000," a take on the popular TV show, *Who Wants To Be a Millionaire.* The game engaged the audience and so impressed Dot Foods that it led to building a client relationship with them. This event also was a special opportunity to express our thanks to all of our clients, our *raison d'être*!

SUCCESSION PLANNING

Business demands were exacting a toll on me, and it was clear that acquiring management talent was the next key issue, a first step toward business succession planning. Quite serendipitously, a good friend, John Sant, who had retired from McDonnell Douglas in 1991, was at our home for dinner in October 1997. He asked if I knew of a company that might need an executive who knew IT.

His friend and former business colleague, F. Mark Kuhlmann, Senior Vice President and General Counsel of McDonnell Douglas, helped John McDonnell negotiate the company's merger with Boeing, but did not want to move to Seattle. He had a background in IT, in addition to his law degree, as he had run the McDonnell Douglas Automation Center for several years. Mark and I met a number of times to talk about SSE, our services, our needs that he could fulfill and simply get to know each other better.

In addition, I had to decide whether or not I was willing to delegate some of the leadership role to someone else. Mark and I reached an understanding that if my daughters were interested in taking over SSE in about 10 years when their family lives were more settled, Mark would be willing to act as a bridge to that eventuality. This was indeed prescient!

I remember calling a mutual friend at McDonnell Douglas, Walter Diggs, as a reference, and he offered, "With your two strong personalities and work ethic, the relationship will either blow up in the first week or it will be a lasting success." It was indeed the latter!

In the final stages of determining that our working relationship would be a good fit, Mark helped me negotiate a successful merger in early 1998 with Productivity Plus, the firm that had backed away from a prior attempt in 1992-1993. It was a reprise of the theme, " ... [the] sin was not in losing, but rather in not winning it back."

As a last step in discussions with Mark about joining SSE, I asked him whether or not he would be able to work in a small business environment. His answer: "I have looked at every aspect of the business in detail and I am comfortable with everything, except that I don't have any way of relating to what it would be like to be in a small business. On that, I am willing to take a chance." He joined SSE as President on April 21, 1998; I became Chairman and CEO. As President, he ran the office day-to-day, functioning as Chief Operating Officer, Chief Financial Officer and General Counsel. This was an exceptional personnel decision for SSE.

■ ■ ■ ■ ■

Through a business acquaintance of his, Mark soon introduced SSE to a rollup/ IPO (Initial Public Offering) venture, ITECH. Our industry was large and growing, yet highly fragmented. The founding companies of ITECH were to number about 10 with aggregate revenues of $150 million to $200 million. The merger was to be consummated simultaneously with the IPO. We explored the idea with a trip in 1998 to New York and a visit to the New York Stock Exchange, but determined that one of the biggest hurdles was whether or not we could generate the revenues to make the merger worthwhile. We decided it was not in our best interest to proceed. The IPO actually never occurred. In hindsight, it was reminiscent of earlier attempts at partnership or merger that began with the Training Matrix about eight years earlier.

TECHNOLOGY-BASED TRAINING ACCELERATES

SSE's growing and dynamic Technology-Based Training (TBT) required expertise in Instructional Design (ID). Led by Nancy Whatley-Blaine, TBT eliminated the cost of a live instructor for each class, instead using a "virtual instructor" on the computer to lead the training. The client just had a one-time upfront training development cost, which was then not only delivered at no cost on an ongoing basis, but also at the convenience of the trainee's time and place. As the training had no classroom boundaries, corporations could generally justify the higher one-time expense.

Enterprise Rent-A-Car, which tapped our early training services in 1987, returned to SSE to develop training for the rollout of its new branch management software system. The training supported a migration from green-screen terminals to custom client/server applications for Enterprise's Rental Fleet Services and Car Sales Remarketing Divisions. It was our first courseware to be delivered on compact disks (CDs). We conceived the practice of hiding "candy" in the courseware as a carrot to entice employees to complete the training. The candy was typically redeemable coupons up to $100 in value. Andy Taylor, CEO and son of the founder, gave high praise to SSE for the training at a conference in California.

LEFT This screen shot of SSE's "Edge" solution for Enterprise-Rent-A-Car shows the "Enterprise Counselor" who acted as a virtual guide through the training program. It was rolled out in 1998 to speed the company's migration from green-screen terminals to automated service in its branches.

ABOVE A Technology-Based Training (TBT) program developed for Bridge Information Systems (later Thomson Reuters) replaced instructor-led sessions and halved training time. The "Game Plan" hockey theme inspired the "20-something" employees with "trading cards," led by the "virtual instructor," to complete the training.

By 1999, we were ready for a game-changing TBT solution for Bridge Information Systems (later Thomson Reuters). Because of the firm's rapid growth, the vice president providing weekly instructor-led training no longer had time for that role. The objective was to automate training on Bridge's financial networks to telephone support personnel while instilling its culture. We attended the class for a week and then developed training that cut training time in half, saving two-and-one-half days per student.

As the training was on a CD (web-based solutions did not yet exist), we could track electronically when a student had successfully completed a training segment, and each completion was rewarded with a "trading card" that told the story of the company and one of its executives for culture reinforcement. The trading cards were such a success that the students ran up and down the halls comparing notes on who had earned what. We had used a hockey theme, meaningful to the "20-something" employees who played on a Bridge ice hockey team after hours. There was such enthusiasm for the "game" that their competitive nature drove the employees to complete the training faster than expected.

This was a "best practice" example of a one-time investment in training that was cost-effective for the long term, especially since the network support work was later outsourced to IBM and then Siemens. The training we developed was used for each transition. Bridge calculated an ROI of seven to one on its training investment. As this was among our first TBT projects, we used it for demonstration purposes for years; it was indeed a "Cadillac" solution!

PREPARATION FOR Y2K

The world began planning in earnest for the Year 2000 (Y2K) transition about 1998. Deloitte & Touche invited me to address its Financial Executives Seminar in late 1997. My topic was, "Year 2000 – The Immovable Date." Subsequently, SSE cosponsored a program alerting St. Louis corporations to the Y2K threat at a session featuring Steve Malphrus of the U.S. Federal Reserve, whom I had met on one of my trips to Washington, D.C., during my tenure on the Fed. More than 200 people attended the program, held at Washington University's Olin School of Business in St. Louis.

We sent letters to clients aimed at helping them prepare for the new millennium. Having learned our lesson to be selective and build upon our core strengths, we elected to adopt a strategy that refused remediation work for companies seeking to modify their old COBOL programs. Our reasoning was twofold: our PC focus meant we had no COBOL programmers, and the liability was immense for projects that didn't make the Y2K transition successfully. While other IT firms were booming with Y2K work, business slowed temporarily for SSE.

Changes wrought by Y2K created immense training opportunities in 1999 for SSE, launching the pinnacle of our instructor-led training and vaulting us worldwide into an international provider. Monsanto elected to transition from CcMail, which was not sufficiently Y2K-compliant, to Microsoft Outlook, and engaged us to train 35,000 people worldwide in a span of three months for the conversion. Our training team members traveled to 23 countries, teaching six classes each day somewhere in the world, around the clock, to complete training before the turn of the new century. As a Microsoft Gold Partner, we were able to use its international training locations and even tap the Microsoft relationship to provide native language training in places where instruction in English was not an option.

Similar training was deployed in 1999 at Ameren for 500 employees and at A.G. Edwards for 600 people in multiple cities. We had four instructors teaching people at Anheuser-Busch, a team at Laclede Gas, plus a Y2K project at The Muny (an outdoor theater in St. Louis that presents Broadway musicals), and expanded training requirements at MasterCard. MasterCard's "Business Across Borders" in 1999 was our Learning Practice's first "soft skills" training engagement. We continued developing custom training for its proprietary clearing system and then its MasterCard Fundamentals.

GOOGLE'S IMPACT

It had not taken long for the Internet to become ubiquitous, advancing from 80,000 hosts in January 1989 to well over 600,000 hosts in more than 100 countries and nearly 5,000 separate networks in 1992. *Computer Reseller News* reported the unit count of Internet access devices at about 30 million to 50 million on November 17, 1996. That count was expected to reach 200 million by 2000.

As the Internet grew exponentially, a new site came online in 1998 with one of the Internet's most simplistic user interfaces: an input box for search criteria and two buttons, one of which still says, "I'm Feeling Lucky." Over the next 10 years, Google, Inc. became the world's most viewed Internet site and was generating $17 billion a year in revenue.

Yet one day's leader can be another day's bygone. Just 12 years after Google's launch, the challenges associated with "nothing as constant as (technological) change" were captured in an August 10, 2010, *Wall Street Journal* story entitled, "Google Agonizes on Privacy as Ad World Vaults Ahead." The basic question, the article said, is, "How far should it [Google] go in profiting from its crown jewels — the vast trove of data it possesses about people's activities?" The article went on to say that " ... the rapid emergence of scrappy rivals who track people's online activities and sell that data, along with Facebook Inc.'s growth, is forcing a shift ... the online ad business is broadening away from Google's sweet spot ... [and has] propelled Internet ad companies into an arms race so swift that even Google fears being left behind."

Six days later, *Fortune Magazine* expanded on the breathtaking pace of change in an article entitled, "Google, The Search Party Is Over." Excerpts included: "The web and the way we use it have changed dramatically ... the web experience is increasingly mobile and social ... Google needs to find real success in this new world — or invent the next major evolution of the web ... Google is not the hot company anymore ... [it's] starting to look like Microsoft and Yahoo! ... [it reflects a] shift going on within the Internet, one that is arguably the biggest change to the web and the way we use it since Google came on the scene ... " This reminded me of IBM's long-lingering, steadfast focus on mainframes instead of acknowledging the role of PCs.

These quotes say it all. They testify dramatically to the pace of change in technology, change that none of us fathomed in the 1960s when the first random access device and Information Retrieval (the Google predecessor) emerged, nor even earlier when IBM predicted in 1958 that there would not be that many computers!

ON THE HOME FRONT

Ironically, our small contribution to the success of Bridge Information Systems helped set the stage for getting booted from our office when Bridge bought the entire building to accommodate its growth. SSE moved in October 1999 to the location it continues to occupy in St. Louis' West Port Plaza. Wendy Gray of Gray Design Group designed our office interior and color scheme to blend our conservative business culture with a high-tech style.

The move was a natural juncture for adopting a new logo. Eric Thoelke of TOKY Design led us through the process of discerning what the logo should communicate and how we would brand the company going forward.

Our logo design was based on Archimedes' axiom, "Give me a fulcrum and a lever, and I will move the world." All the logo components were open-ended to imply that the world was wide open to us. We decided to focus on branding the company as SSE, using Systems Service Enterprises, Inc. only for business and contractual purposes. Eric also encouraged us to capitalize "SSE" in our website address, www.SSEinc.com, to further emphasize our brand.

LEFT SSE adopted its current logo in 1999. The design was based on Archimedes' axiom, "Give me a fulcrum and a lever, and I will move the world."

a new CENTURY

The Y2K threat was resolved by the dawn of the new millennium. It paved the way for an IT newcomer known euphemistically as the dot-com bubble. The "build it and they will come" assumption of the dot-com bubble that followed preparations for Y2K did not fit with our conservative approach to business. New dot-com enterprises were eager to spread their risk to the organization developing the application for the elusive promise of sharing in the reward. It was a position we were unwilling to take most of the time, and it proved to be a fortunate business call. Most of the startups burst quickly and were out of business before generating cash flow and profits.

For example, we partnered with Influence LLC, a new age marketing firm founded by serial entrepreneur, Craig Kaminer, on two dot-com bubble apps: Sell Meat, an auction-based site where customers would bid on meat online (from which we did receive payment), and Haystack Toys. Haystack's Great American Toy Hunt, a public relations extravaganza that traveled from city to city in search of new toys and collected ideas through its website, never caught on (and never paid us). Neither site ever attained success. Atisma Technologies, with its web-based management software for K-12 schools, higher education and nonprofits, also floundered and left us holding the bag.

SUCCESSFUL INITIATIVES

One leading-edge supply chain initiative that was deemed a great success by its owner, John Ross, was for his office products company, Indoff. He selected SSE to build a system that entailed a totally automated solution from order entry to customer delivery. It was a far cry from my first order entry system for Monsanto in 1960. The app accepted orders online, performed an automatic search to find the closest distribution center to the customer, developed all the required picking and shipping tickets, and then automatically drop-shipped the order to its customer. Ellen Bohn created this sophisticated web app in 1998, another leading-edge solution with complex data entry using SQL Server, version 6.5. SSE's team also delivered CD-based training for the nationwide sales force to accompany the software release.

■ ■ ■ ■ ■

Dot Foods, Inc., impressed with our Windows 2000 rollout, engaged SSE to develop its online inventory access solution. Kevin Grossnicklaus (whom we dubbed "G" because we had three employees named Kevin) worked closely with Microsoft and Dot Foods to develop one of the Midwest's first production ASP. NET-based eCommerce sites. The site was later recognized by Microsoft as an early adopter case study. G was the expert on the beta versions of ASP+ and the Next Generation of Web Services platform, and his case study was included in Microsoft's regional launch of the .NET Framework kit.

Dot Foods, the nation's leading food redistributor, with headquarters in Mt. Sterling, Illinois, needed a major overhaul to make it faster and easier for customers to do business with the company. They wanted to give customers direct inventory access, a model that reduced distributors' inventory costs and warehouse space. Our solution also featured order-fulfillment capabilities to enable distributors to complete the supply chain. Upon going live in November 2001, Dot Foods increased its total monthly online orders by 182.4 percent and won about 250 new customers. The number of searches conducted on the site increased 128 percent, a critical indicator of the success of its online business.

During the development, we trained some of Dot Foods' software developers at desks in our office so they could effectively be part of the team. G was the leader and visionary in the creation of this application, continuing to head a team to redesign and develop enhancements for years afterward.

Shortly after the launch, we won the Best B-to-B (Business-to-Business) Site award in the food industry for DotExpressway.com in 2002. It was a great win from *B-to-B Magazine* with stiff competition! As of 2008, www.DotExpressway.com was still processing millions of dollars of orders every year.

■ ■ ■ ■ ■

Another award winner under G's leadership was a website designed and developed for the Greater St. Louis Area Council of the Boy Scouts of America in 2002. It leveraged Microsoft's Content Management Server product to automate updating and distribution of its web content. In 2004, the Council received the Boy Scouts of America National President's Award for Marketing Excellence.

TEAM GROWTH & REFINEMENT

A series of internal changes, combined with business and talent acquisitions, helped us keep pace with the demands of the ever-changing technology world.

A key management addition was Tom Wyman, who joined SSE at the turn of the century as Vice President - Technology and Delivery. With Tom at the helm, we combined all of our technical services into one delivery force. By this time, JY (who had joined SSE in 1986 as VP – Finance and Technical Services) was focused on the financial side of the business. This internal consolidation streamlined service delivery and reinforced SSE's "customer sat" philosophy in serving our clients.

We also introduced the concept of "practice leaders" to better retain our critical focus on technical expertise. Our practice leaders approach was an antidote to the silos we had inadvertently encouraged by keeping separate Profit & Loss (P&L) records for each practice area. While useful for tracking the profitability of each area of our business, the downsides were numerous. Among them were failure to capitalize on cross-selling, creating gaps in service to our clients and reluctance among practices to share employees for fear they would be unavailable when needed, even if our internal charge-back system allowed each employee's resident silo to get partial credit for the work. What a kludge process!

UPWARD SPIRAL

Boeing, a longtime client, engaged SSE for two months to backfill its user support needs as it planned a move from Unix to Microsoft Windows 2000. Vince Sechrest, the project lead and now our Network Services Practice Leader, and his team had exceeded Boeing's expectations. The reward: Boeing asked us to lead the conversion of its 1,200 workstations to Windows 2000. We were able to reduce the average migration time from 12 hours per system to just two hours, a sixfold productivity gain. We are proud to say that our relationship-driven approach has continued to work as Boeing engages us today.

Vince also led the team that performed the Microsoft Active Directory design and development for Charter Communications. Active Directory (AD) was a directory service first released by Microsoft with its Windows 2000 Server edition, using standardized protocols to provide a variety of network services. Implementation of this first-to-market product continued our commitment to leading-edge solutions.

The Boeing engagement and our network successes made it clear internally that SSE's technical skills were strong enough to be proactive in further serving the needs of our clients. We introduced an evolutionary version of our Peak Performance Agreements, the Technology Management System (TMS) program, whereby network engineers performed regularly scheduled visits to clients each month and manually completed a checklist. It is hard to believe this was a new idea! This literally provided the learning experience that helped formulate Vince's vision of proactively recognizing clients' needs and preventing accidents from happening with the ultimate launch of Pretecht in 2005.

■ ■ ■ ■ ■

Just as SSE had learned to stick to core strengths, we became the beneficiary when others arrived at similar conclusions. On January 1, 2001, we merged PureLogix into SSE, the software development division founded by Rob Topping of Westar. He had decided it no longer fit with his business strategy and approached me the prior fall. With the acquisition came some special employees, including Kevin Queen, another Practice Leader whose nickname quickly became "Q," and an outstanding business practice at Boeing in Embedded Systems Development. Essentially the team wrote software that was placed on a chip implemented in specific hardware. Among other projects, they wrote the software that made the JDAM (Joint Direct Attack Munition) Bomb smart! The PureLogix engineers also expanded SSE's software development capability to Java and Oracle.

During 2002, we acquired Partec's IT consulting business from CSI Leasing when founder Ken Steinback likewise determined the need for a sole focus, leasing mainframes. It was a good fit for us to assume Partec's contracts and employees.

It is intriguing to contrast this with the years when IBM leased its own mainframes. Here the sales were outsourced to CSI, who in turn leased the systems back to the client. The practice was also a throwback to my Centerre days, when the bank bought barges and corporate aircraft for the investment tax credit under the U.S. Revenue Act of 1971, and then leased the equipment back to customers.

The acquisitions were each win-wins. Since PureLogix and Partec technical support had become a distraction for its founders, the changes allowed them to gain focus while finding a solid home for trusted employees. Clients received uninterrupted service with familiar personnel, and SSE acquired new business, new clients and great new talent. Parenthetically, when Elizabeth spun off our application development group in mid-2009 to sharpen SSE's focus, she found a home for all our employees with Oakwood Systems Group, Inc.

BUSINESS INTELLIGENCE

Ellen Bohn stepped up once again to create a new type of solution, Business Intelligence (BI). It was a repeat project with Maverick Tube, as we continued to be blessed with ongoing clients. The concept of BI was to gather data, such as "sales by territory," and present the data in a cube or matrix format on the business user's desktop. Then the user could drill down through the levels of data to a specific person in a targeted geography. The system updated the data each night, so it was always current.

Initially, Maverick asked us to survey and analyze the BI software on the market, such as Hyperion and Business Objects, each of which cost in the neighborhood of $500,000 for a corporate license. We suggested we could develop a solution that would meet their needs at a fraction of the price using Excel Pivot Tables, already available on everyone's PC in the Microsoft suite of products. The app used SQL Server 2000 and Oracle 8.0i and met their needs for several years. The desktop cubes that Ellen developed were lauded by Maverick as the best data design its IT department had ever delivered.

In fact, the "cobbler's children" got an oar in edgewise as we modified the app for ourselves to provide SSE managers with access to current sales and development data, benefitting once more from our client-driven solutions. Further, we modified the app, branded it SSExcelerator, and sold it to Angelica and Aurora Foods, to name a few.

BI, along with eLearning, subsequently became the hot service offerings of the day. One BI tool was Crystal Reports, business intelligence software used to design and generate reports from a wide range of data sources, such as initially linking dBASE and Paradox data. McDonnell Douglas engaged SSE to develop a "how to" guide to using Crystal Reports. Lisa Olenski, better known as "Lisa O." because we had two employees named Lisa, developed the courseware that we were later given permission to sell to other companies. Element K, which by coincidence had acquired Ziff Communications in 2000, ultimately acquired the rights to sell our courseware, which produced a nice source of royalty income for years. In a sense, the royalty concept might have been another way to create "annuity" revenue, a concept of ongoing revenue streams identified later by Elizabeth, but it also could have become an out-of-focus distraction. No matter! It was a nice dividend each month.

9/11

With the tech world consumed by Y2K and then the dot-com bubble, the changes they precipitated paled by comparison to September 11, 2001, a day that will live in our hearts and minds forever. Just as had happened when President John F. Kennedy was assassinated, nearly all Americans can remember exactly where they were upon learning of the tragedy, stretching from the twin towers of the World Trade Center in New York City, to the Pentagon in Washington, D.C., to a field in Pennsylvania.

As a gift to the American Red Cross, we wrote a commemorative online Flash video to be used as a tribute and thank-you to volunteers who helped in the St. Louis 9/11 effort and to drive continued donations for unfinished work. Singer Sarah McLachlan granted permission for us to use her song, *"I Will Remember You,"* free for three months. It was a poignant message in light of the more than 3,000 lives lost, with the refrain:

I will remember you

Will you remember me?

Don't let your life pass you by

Weep not for the memories.

The tragedy permanently changed our American culture. 9/11 also precipitated a sea change in our training practice. Due to new transportation security constraints, corporations no longer wanted to put their people on planes to deliver or attend instructor-led training. We were ready for the change, having experimented with other forms of TBT (Technology-Based Training) courseware, as CD-based projects, such as Bridge, had become passé. A web-based solution was the leading-edge next step, allowing corporations to deliver their training globally without the perceived danger, cost or delays in travel.

unabated
CHANGE

Blended Learning/eLearning was again front-and-center in SSE's services portfolio as world events merged new service concepts with emerging technology to meet clients' needs in a global business environment in 2002.

eLEARNING COMES INTO ITS OWN

SSE's first big eLearning client was Humana. The application coached Humana's contract experts on effectively negotiating contracts in the new era of regulations, such as the Health Insurance Portability and Accountability Act (HIPAA) of 1996. Although there were only about 250 negotiators, Humana justified the expense of the eLearning system by the results. Each negotiator was able to save millions of dollars per contract by virtue of the web-delivered training. Mary Hamlin was our key client contact and she helped usher in a new era at Humana. By the way, the Humana opportunity resulted from a cold call by our account executive, Kevin Gregory, whose nickname, you guessed it, was "G2."

The courseware development process created by Brenda Enders and her team from the beginning was to partner with our clients to tap into the intimate business knowledge of their own Subject Matter Experts (SMEs). We brought to the table the ability to assess and understand their business and learning objectives, plus the Instructional Design (ID) expertise to create the appropriate courseware. Today, we call this "collaborship" (collaboration + partnership).

Humana accessed the web-based contract negotiations training through the newly created SSElearn Portal[SM], SSE's proprietary Learning Management System (LMS). In addition to delivering the training as if it were on Humana's website, it tracked the students and what courses they had taken, and delivered detailed statistics about each learner, such as course completion data.

LMSs had begun to appear on the market for companies to store their eLearning courseware on servers to manage online course content, the learners and the delivery process. If they had not already made the investment, it was more cost-effective for our clients to use SSE's portal rather than be charged for the extra time to develop and implement another LMS. Clients also chose to use SSE's portal if they required programming features that enhanced the educational experience but were not compliant with the industry standards, AICC/SCORM. (AICC is an acronym for Aviation Industry Computer-Based Training Committee, an international association of technology-based training professionals that develops training guidelines for the aviation industry, and SCORM stands for Sharable Content Object Reference Model.)

SSE also was selected to develop diversity and change management eLearning for Sears' 34,000 midlevel managers. Our Sears client-partner team won the highly coveted internal Quality Award for the project.

PRODUCT LAUNCH VIA eLEARNING

Shortly thereafter, Brenda and crew were on a roll as SSE competitively won a major contract with Avon Products, Inc. to develop all the online training content and delivery of its new "mark." product line, targeting 16- to 24-year-olds. Avon's objective was to attract a new generation of sales representatives in the same age bracket as those targeted by the new product through the Internet to match that age group's favored communications venue. The web-based training was a fun and flashy way for new sales reps to learn about Avon's products, access

sales training, order marketing supplies, fulfill orders, manage their money and set up their own businesses.

At the conclusion of the course work, each student completed a 36-hour self-guided online exercise to create a business plan that was submitted to Avon for review. This was a significant milestone for Avon, marking the first time in its history to have one-on-one communication with sales representatives. The courseware was articulated to meet the University of Phoenix's requirements, as an Avon rep completing the course and writing the requisite business plan was awarded 1.5 college credits from Phoenix. Learning was integrated with a fulfillment house to send rewards to students based on completion of training segments, another application of our "candy" concept introduced earlier for Enterprise Rent-A-Car.

Avon went live with its sales training for "mark." representatives in 2003. With the largest sales force in the world, plus the new students, more than 100,000 hits per day were logged on the SSElearn Portal! Avon remained on our portal for several years until negotiating with us to take it in-house. In retrospect, this was not a new occurrence. Time and again, training and PC support were taken in-house by clients when sufficient internal mastery was developed to reduce delivery costs.

With Avon and Humana as the first of many major clients to host their content within our LMS, our SSElearn Portal grew and evolved. It was always transparent to the learner, as users accessed our portal through their own website. Besides being a real value-add to the client, it was also one of our first true "annuity" revenue-generation opportunities, as clients used our LMS on a contract basis.

As an aside, we viewed our connection with the University of Phoenix as an opportunity to move SSE into the university eLearning environment. We explored relationships with other university online learning companies, and it became clear that the Instructional Design (ID) and delivery methods of our corporate expertise were entirely different from the university online courseware world. Once again, we determined it was prudent to stay with what we knew rather than distracting ourselves in a realm we didn't know.

GOVERNMENT FORAY

In 2004, we were engaged for an especially meaningful eLearning project for the U.S. Army Maneuver Support Center of Excellence in Fort Leonard Wood, Missouri. The goal was to provide instruction and assessment training to our troops going to Iraq for spotting and neutralizing bombs, mines and booby traps.

The concept was articulated in a *St. Louis Post-Dispatch* article on Sunday, September 19, 2004: "The goal is to make it as realistic as possible ... soldiers can go through a city in Iraq and touch a garbage can and it can explode ... they can be injured by shrapnel or lose an arm. It's an out-of-box approach to training ... Ultimately, this solution will save lives."

With this first government experience under our belts, we were selected in 2006 to develop the First Responder basic chemistry training program for the U.S. Army Chemical, Biological, Radiological and Nuclear (CBRN) School, also at Fort Leonard Wood. Our training taught new recruits how to respond to crisis situations, such as fire or explosions. We developed 50 hours of courseware that included effective simulations of real-life situations.

■ ■ ■ ■ ■

Our continued efforts to pursue government business and build on these Fort Leonard Wood successes led us to Scott Air Force Base across the Mississippi River from St. Louis near Belleville, Illinois. At an Illinois outreach program sponsored by the Regional Business Council (RBC), I had the privilege of meeting Gen. John W. Handy, the Four-Star General at Scott Air Force Base and Commander of the U.S. Transportation Command (USTRANSCOM). Gen. Handy developed the concept of centralizing global logistics for the U.S. Department of Defense, including outsourcing to private transportation

ABOVE LEFT In 2004, SSE developed its first government eLearning for American troops going to Iraq. Completed for the U.S. Army Manueuver Support Center of Excellence in Fort Leonard Wood, Missouri, it helped troops learn how to "virtually" spot and neutralize bombs, mines and booby traps using a mouse-driven pointer. **ABOVE RIGHT** SSE won an opportunity with the U.S. Transportation Command at Scott Air Force Base in 2007 to describe its mission in an online video. This screen shot tells USTRANSCOM's story in a quote from former Secretary of Defense Donald Rumsfeld.

companies. He was responsible for the movement of personnel, equipment and supplies by air, land and sea anywhere in the world in the most cost-effective manner, depending on the urgency of receipt. USTRANSCOM also responded to humanitarian crises and even provided transportation for the U.S. President on Air Force One. Its mantra was "Factory to Foxhole."

Summoning my courage as I went through the event receiving line, I asked him for help in getting business at Scott. In the process of calling on the base, I had several opportunities to meet with Gen. Handy and he is the one who reinforced for me the importance of perseverance. I remember asking him, "What do I have to do to get business at Scott?" His answer was, "If it is important to you and your company, you must be persistent." It was and we did! He has remained a great friend and mentor since his retirement in September 2005.

Thanks to his great advice about perseverance, Brenda Enders and her team scored again with the government. We were engaged in 2007 by USTRANSCOM to develop an informational piece to tell the base's story, entitled "DPO Awareness." The first screen of the piece showed a quote from former Secretary of Defense Donald Rumsfeld, dated September 16, 2003: "The Commander, U.S. Transportation Command, is designated as the Distribution Process

Owner (DPO). The DPO shall improve overall efficiency and interoperability of distribution-related activities — deployment, sustainment, redeployment support during peace and war." We were especially proud of this win!

SPECIAL RECOGNITIONS

SSE began to draw notice from many quarters, first winning the regional Mississippi Valley Business of the Year Award in 2002 from Southern Illinois University-Edwardsville. While it was an honor to be recognized for overall business excellence, the proof of our value to clients' business performance was in the industry awards highlighting our leading-edge solutions.

It was gratifying to have SSE's outstanding work recognized with a series of international awards beginning in the fall of 2004, when we won our first award from Brandon Hall Research (the global authority in the workplace eLearning world). Since 1999, its Excellence in Learning Awards program had been recognizing the best in innovative workplace learning content, technology and initiatives. We were awarded a gold medal in the Custom Content, Full Course Category, for our Avon's "mark." Blended Learning solution. This award ranked SSE's solutions among the top five percent in the world!

The next year we won a bronze medal from Brandon Hall Research in the Custom Content, Full Course Category, for our web-based solution on "Controlling Unemployment Costs" for TALX. This was SSE's first initiative based on "contextualized" learning, simulating learners' workplace environment and experiences. Back-to-back awards within the same category remain an extremely rare occurrence.

The SSE eLearning team next won an international APEX Award for Publication in 2007, recognizing the eLearning sales training program used for new employee orientation at AAA Missouri. In 2008, the team was recognized for the electronic-fulfillment warehousing curriculum developed for forklift operators at Bunzl Distribution USA, Inc., and in 2009, for our contextualized order fulfillment software curriculum, working closely with our Bunzl clients, Ken Aull and Peggy Nance.

The team's award-winning streak continued in 2010 when SSE's RehabCare mobile computing solution for its therapists and program directors won the Chief Learning Officer (CLO) Learning in Practice Merit Award and another international APEX Award for implementing training on RehabCare's new point-of-service device, the Apple iPod Touch and iPhone.

SSE's RehabCare project, our first experience with developing for the mobile technology world, was the latest expression of our passion for delivering leading-edge solutions. It also ushered SSE into the "mLearning" world, the next stage of "eLearning."

"The Year in Review: Mobile Technology," a *Wall Street Journal* article on December 28, 2010, stated: " ... the computer truly went mobile ... smartphones plunged into the mainstream, giving millions of people the ability to browse the Internet ... without having to sit down and boot up a laptop." Another *Wall Street Journal* article on March 24, 2011, said: "The flood of venture capital into mobile social startups is the latest sign of Silicon Valley's web-fueled boom ... What's different now is the ubiquity of smartphones and tablets." As noted so many times, this simply continued the dramatic pace of change from PCs to the Internet and now social networking on cell phones.

In a span of just six years, each of these award-winning solutions was completely leading-edge for its time, from web-based to mobile computing!

SUCCESSION COMPLETE

Elizabeth Elliott Niedringhaus became President of SSE in April 2004. After nearly nine years of ever-broadening responsibility and success in sales and marketing, leading our Solutions Division (infrastructure and custom software development), and then serving as Vice President of Business Development, there was no doubt that she had earned the entire team's confidence. The succession plan that originated with hiring former McDonnell Douglas executive Mark Kuhlmann as President in 1998 had worked. Mark and I became co-CEOs and I continued as Chairman. We also hired Jim Dobbins as our Chief Financial Officer, as Elizabeth was beginning to build her team.

When I announced her appointment to the whole company, I noted that Enterprise Rent-A-Car and Maritz, two well-known St. Louis companies and both clients of SSE, had been taken to enormous heights by the second-generation leaders. That was my vision and dream for Elizabeth as well. I knew she and her team could do it!

■ ■ ■ ■ ■

Elizabeth formed a Hedgehog Council of her team, composed of key employees in both the sales and service delivery areas, but not including Mark and me. Instead she reported on its progress monthly to the two of us.

The council was based on a concept that Jim Collins described in his book, *Good to Great*. Council members explored Collins' thesis on focusing your business by asking three key questions:

1. What can you be best in the world at?
2. What are you deeply passionate about?
3. What best drives your economic engine?

The Hedgehog Council defined our mission and vision as follows, reflecting that the best never changes:

MISSION: We improve the performance of our clients' organizations by managing and improving the flow of information and knowledge.

VISION: Through a commitment to client partnership built on delivering consistently high quality, value-based solutions, services and products, SSE is recognized as the market leader in technology and education.

A perennial challenge with a technical workforce in a project-oriented business remained bench-time management. Closely timing the deployment of a requisite set of skills between one project's completion and the next one's start is nearly impossible to manage, creating a gap that saps business profitability. Elizabeth intensified her drive for developing "annuity" services to address this issue. The council brainstormed more than 100 ideas, electing to concentrate on two major initiatives, both of which held promise for balancing SSE's project-based business revenue with contract-based "annuity" commitments:

- Learning Content Aggregation, building further upon the SSElearn Portal introduced in 2002.
- Development of a Managed Network Services product, TMS2 (Technology Management Services 2), code-named Tomacco after an episode of *The Simpsons*. It ultimately became Pretecht[SM] (preventive technology), a proactive service for network management, technical support and IT maintenance.

LEFT SSE launched the beta version of its "first-to-market" Pretecht product in 2005, aimed at helping small businesses without in-house IT capabilities prevent IT problems and failures through predictive network monitoring and proactive response. © Callaway & Company, designed by Sarah Bowman, Bowman Design.

ANNUITY PRODUCTS

In the realm of Learning Content Aggregation, our SSElearn Portal had been designed and first deployed to deliver Humana's training in 2002 and was used again for Avon in 2003. With Brenda and her team's vision for the eLearning group and the expertise of our application development group, led by Kevin "G" Grossnicklaus, the teams continued to collaborate to enable delivery of learning solutions using the SSElearn Portal, driving annuity revenue.

The Tomacco vision combined our network management services practice with our custom development expertise to execute the design and implementation of a network monitoring and management software system. When the beta version launched in 2005 as Pretecht, it was a "first-to-market" product! Under the leadership of Vince Sechrest, the network requirements were defined from his years of network experience, and G once again envisioned the application development solution. With these two key leaders under one roof and across the hall from each other, as was true of the SSElearn Portal team, the "cobbler's children" demonstrated they were leaders, not laggards, by accomplishing the projects totally in-house.

Pretecht, our second source of "annuity" revenues, was designed to assist small businesses lacking in-house IT capabilities. Its name conveyed proactivity, preventive maintenance and protective services in the management of clients' business systems. This revolutionary approach managed clients' networks remotely and predicted issues and impending failures before they caused downtime or, worse yet, the loss of data. For instance, the system could remotely predict that a hard drive was filling up and on the verge of crashing. The ability to then plan an off-hours replacement created client savings by eliminating lost-time work hours for client staff and avoiding both data losses and crisis response expenses. We restored our 24-hour support desk to drive Pretecht's remote monitoring and servicing capabilities, and SSE's network clients tripled in the next year.

Within five years, the network services industry began its transition to "cloud computing" in 2009. In the category of déjà vu or "what goes around comes around," IBM's Service Bureaus had functioned as "cloud computing" resources by hosting corporate systems in a centralized fashion on mainframes in the late 1960s and early 1970s. By 2010, cloud computing had become a way to centralize the hosting of apps for companies in server centers, accessed over the Internet and utilizing leading-edge data storage technology.

SSE's "cloud" strategy focused on helping clients assess where the cloud fit best into their overall business/IT strategy, both short- and long-term. Our website read: "Perhaps the best solution will be a 'hybrid solution' where some of your IT services will move to the cloud, while others will remain 'on-premise' as they have been traditionally. Let SSE help you find the right fit for your business – request a 'Cloud Fitness Assessment' today!"

SMART CLIENT CONTAINER

In addition to leading the full-scale launch of Pretecht in 2006, G, then our Enterprise Application Architect (who now has his own company, ArchitectNow), recognized the potential for Smart Client applications and began developing the SSE Smart Client Container[SM] (SCC) product in earnest. The SCC, also known as "WinEngine," was a powerful user-interface "shell" and framework on which developers could build robust, Windows-based Smart Client applications using the .NET Framework. Unlike other framework products, the SCC provided a sound set of services, or tools, such as the low-level classes and services needed by developers, to help provide capabilities and enforce best practices. It also provided a user-interface container that hosted new functionality, such as highly extensible add-in architecture to permit development teams to "plug in" new features.

SSE launched the proprietary app in 2006 with a national web initiative, marking the culmination of an effort that began in 2003 to research, develop, license and package this type of custom software. With the SSElearn Portal and Pretecht products, our Smart Client Container emerged as the third software "product" in which we invested and developed ourselves.

Using this innovation as a base, SSE created a broker desktop solution now called Lipper for Investment Managers (LIM). Lipper, a global supplier of mutual fund information, was then a recently purchased subsidiary of Reuters who, in turn, was a successor to Bridge Information Systems (and has since been acquired by Thomson Reuters). Using the SSE Smart Client Container, the LIM app provided a rich client interface for brokers around the world to access and analyze massive amounts of secure mutual fund information. Lipper rolled out the product to more than 3,000 fund managers across the world, earning client praise for bringing its vision for a new fund analysis program to life within an aggressive timeframe.

SMOTHER PROGRAM

Riding high on the success of our SSElearn, Pretecht and Smart Client Container product breakthroughs, we initiated a service-oriented project after the discovery of several client issues. My old IBM training underscored ways to "smother" our customers with attention and ensure they were satisfied with our solutions. That hearkened back to the days when IBM's systems engineering services were free under the mainframe hardware lease. It was equally important 50 years later.

Client service remained as essential to business vitality in 2011 as innovation and technological development were to the future of the business. There is no alternative, especially in a service business! Just as our willingness to unbox PCs and install them to meet a need expressed by Mary Berthold at Monsanto had initiated a new SSE service in 1985, the constant enculturation of our staff in the SMOTHER concepts kept our service culture alive and spawning new innovations. After multiple meetings with our key technical employees, we rolled out the SMOTHER program to the whole team:

S	Services
M	Make SSE the best choice
O	Overwhelm our clients with knowledge and understanding
T	Trusted technology partner
H	Help them solve business problems to transform their business
E	Exceed their expectations
R	Relationships built to last

REFLECTIONS ON
civic
OUTREACH

As I was resuming operations for SSE in 1983, other women across the nation were organizing in varied ways to forge new ground. One such initiative was the Missouri Women's Forum, an affiliate of the International Women's Forum, founded in St. Louis by Virginia E. Masters, cofounder of the Masters and Johnson Institute. I felt fortunate to be a charter member.

I had been privileged to gain opportunities to serve on a variety of boards through the years for organizations seeking a token woman. Having gained access simply because I was a woman, I tried to go above and beyond in every case to make a difference. Each board experience led to other invitations where a token was needed. While I heard a number of women moan and groan about how they were treated as second-class citizens and insinuate an entitlement to special treatment, I really felt they did a disservice to the rest of us who worked hard and earned our recognition.

An article published in the *St. Louis Post-Dispatch* by Repps Hudson on August 29, 2008, recognizing SSE's 25th anniversary and entitled "Chairman of SSE Inc. does things her way," told the story: " ... her title ... is 'chairman,' not 'chair' or 'chairwoman.' Although Elliott clearly was a trailblazer who established her career and company in a male-dominated time and field ... [50] years ago, she has had no inclination to declare that to the world. She preferred instead to let her deeds speak for themselves."

To reflect on the feminine mystique subject, following are two quotes, 50 years apart, that cover the position of women in organizations:

- In an article I wrote for the St. Louis Chapter Data Processing Management Association while at IBM, entitled "Women in Data Processing," I said that women "provide the detailed technical backup for proposal presentations and demonstrations." It was obvious that a direct sales job was not a consideration, and yet the conclusion of the article read: "Wherever there is data processing equipment or a related product or service, today [1964] you are as likely to encounter a woman as a man." George Conrades, an IBM salesman in that era, confirmed that they could neither complete a sale nor the subsequent implementation without the women because we dotted the i's and crossed the t's to make it a success.

- Almost 50 years later, the same issue was reflected in a *New York Times* article on April 18, 2010, entitled, "Out of the Loop in Silicon Valley ... In the Wide-Open World of Tech, So Few Women?" It noted "a stark imbalance of the sexes persists in the high-tech world, where change typically happens at breakneck speed ... substantial barriers still confront women trying to scale the technological peaks."

GROWING INFLUENCE

In 1996, I had been appointed to a five-year term as a director of the Federal Reserve Bank of St. Louis, serving as Deputy Chairman for three years and Chairman for two years. It was an awesome opportunity to meet and work with Alan Greenspan at a critical time in our economy. It was the period leading up to the Year 2000 and the dot-com bubble, identified by Alan Greenspan as one of "irrational exuberance." During this time, the increase in productivity with technology and the Internet's ubiquity spurred major policy implications and economic impact.

ABOVE Susan Elliott served on the Federal Reserve Bank of St. Louis Board of Directors from 1996-2000 while Alan Greenspan (left) was Chairman of the Fed. As Deputy Chairman for three years and then Chairman of the Board for two years, she attended the Conference of Chairmen twice a year in Washington, D.C. Photograph by Scott Raffe.

After my service at the Fed, Ameren Corp. CEO Chuck Mueller approached me about joining the board of Angelica, a linen and uniform company (today focused solely on health care linen services). A good friend and my successor as Fed chairman, Chuck opened the door to my first public board experience. Several years later, thanks to Chuck and Peter MacCarthy, an Ameren director, I was invited to join the Ameren Board, the public utility in Missouri and Illinois. Angelica was taken private in 2006 and I resigned from Ameren in 2010, having reached the mandatory retirement age of 72.

In that same period, I served on the nonprofit boards of the St. Louis Zoological Foundation as well as the St. Louis Science Center, on which I remain today. Other board terms were served at Webster University with campuses worldwide, the St. Louis Regional Chamber and Growth Association (RCGA) and the Regional Business Council (RBC). As a founding member of the RBC, we worked closely with its first and current director, Kathy Osborn.

In a focused effort aimed at helping St. Louis attract technology businesses, I helped found the Technology Gateway Alliance in the late 1990s. In 2006, Dr. William A. Peck, along with civic leaders and the RCGA, announced the successor to the alliance, Innovate St. Louis, to enhance the region's entrepreneurial environment and catalyze the region's emergence as a global hub of innovation and entrepreneurship.

"Innovate St. Louis will be a high-level organization, limited in size, transforming in mission and flexible in implementation," Peck noted. "It will sponsor multiple activities, which alone and in partnership with others, will provide unique contributions to a strong vital entrepreneurial culture in our community." A great lesson reinforced was that civic outreach and the opportunity to network are absolutely essential in business "rainmaking."

The *St. Louis Business Journal* began honoring successful women in 1999 with its "Most Influential Business Women" recognition, and I was privileged to be in the first group so honored. Fast forward to 2010, my daughter, Elizabeth Elliott Niedringhaus, was named a "Most Influential Business Woman." We became St. Louis' first mother/daughter combo to be recognized in this way.

OPPOSITE Elizabeth Elliott Niedringhaus, who was 14 when her mother founded SSE in 1983, was named to the *St. Louis Business Journal's* list of Most Influential Business Women in 2010. She and Susan, who had been in the first group of women recognized in 1999, became the first mother-daughter combination to have received the honor.

MOST INFLUENTIAL: The region's top business women

St. Louis Business Journal

VOL. 30, NO. 51   56 PAGES   stlouis.bizjournals.com   August 13-19, 2010 $2.00

Elizabeth NIEDRINGHAUS
SSE Inc.

SSE Inc. is opening its first out-of-town office in Jacksonville, Fla., a move Elizabeth Niedringhaus is overseeing.

"We have six people on the ground now, and we'll be fully operational by the end of September with 30 employees," said Niedringhaus, 41, president and CEO of the technology and education firm.

The Jacksonville office will boost the head count of the Westport-area technology company by a third, up from 89 people in 2009.

Since taking over as SSE's president in 2004, Niedringhaus has been shifting the direction of the business founded by her mother, Susan Elliot, chairman of the company.

A year ago, the company sold its software application development division to another local technology firm, Oakwood Systems. SSE already had dropped its contract staffing business. Niedringhaus said the changes allow SSE to focus on its faster-growing lines of business — learning services and network services.

"When I think of Elizabeth Niedringhaus, the words 'strategic' and 'focus' come to mind," said Andrew Hereford, president of Parkside Financial Bank & Trust Co., which named her to its board. "Before she came aboard SSE, the company was in a handful of businesses. Some did well, some not so well. She took a hard look at what the company's core competencies were and where its future was."

Hereford said Niedringhaus does the same on Parkside's board, holding the bank's management accountable to focusing on its core competencies. She brings another plus to the table, he said: "She knows technologies, and she helps develop our technologies."

Niedringhaus had no plans to join the business after college and moved to San Francisco. That changed in 1995, when her mother recruited her for a sales position. Niedringhaus has been rising through the ranks ever since. In 2004, she was named to the *St. Louis Business Journal*'s "40 under 40" when she was SSE's vice president of business development, several months before she was named president. In being named to this year's Most Influential Business Women, she joins her mother, who was named to the 1999 class.

Niedringhaus, 41, also is president of the St. Louis Chapter of the Entrepreneur's Organization for the 2010-11 term. She is a member of the St. Louis Regional Business Council and the board of Mary Institute and Saint Louis Country Day School. Niedringhaus resigned earlier this year from the Saint Louis Zoo board after four years with the organization to devote more time to her business, family and other volunteer activities.

— Rick Desloge

Inspirational

Learning about this year's class of Most Influential Business Women has been jaw-droppingly inspirational.

This extraordinary and diverse group — which includes educators, lawyers, IT executives, accountants and financiers — makes an impact not only on St. Louis, but also around the world.

We even have a military connection in Brig. Gen. Michelle Johnson of USTRANSCOM. Imagine coordinating global military personnel and equipment while parenting twin 7-year-old boys. Which would be more challenging?

St. Louis' Most Influential Business Women are CEOs, presidents, vice presidents, managers, leaders, mothers, daughters, sisters and wives, but each is influential in her own way. Get to know them by reading their 25 profiles in the following pages.

And thanks, as always, to our sponsors: UMSL, PNC Bank, Armstrong Teasdale and Deloitte.

-Chris Bergeron Linton, Section editor

25 years of
LEADING-EDGE SOLUTIONS
& 50 years in
TECHNOLOGY

CHAPTER 16

In September 2008, SSE hosted a major celebration for two extraordinary reasons. We marked 25 years, 1983 to 2008, of providing leading-edge technology solutions to clients worldwide in the PC arena, a niche no one thought would ever support a business. And we celebrated my 50 years in technology since going to work for IBM in 1958.

Wrapping up these 50-plus years, Elizabeth succeeded me as CEO in 2010. She is President and CEO; I remain as Chairman. Mark Kuhlmann left day-to-day participation in the business in early 2008, 10 years after he came to us as the bridge to a point in time at which one of my daughters might want to run SSE. Our oldest daughter, Kathryn Elliott Love, my raison d'être for starting SSE, is a Partner in the law firm of Bryan Cave LLP in St. Louis, an SSE board member and SSE's legal counsel. Lastly, our one other board member is my husband, Howard Elliott, Jr., without whom I could never have made it through these past 50 years. He has been my greatest support system in the world!

TOP Susan with Howard Elliott, Jr., her husband, whom she credits as the "greatest support system in the world." © Olan Mills, Inc., April 2009. **BOTTOM** Susan Elliott (center) with her daughters, Elizabeth Elliott Niedringhaus (left), who succeeded Susan as SSE President and CEO, and Kathryn Elliott Love, Susan's *raison d'être* in 1966 for incorporating SSE.

What follows is a postscript that Elizabeth has written, reflecting our current standing in the tech world through the team effort of mother and daughter. I am truly blessed to have her take over so successfully and run the business without skipping a beat.

POSTSCRIPT

by Elizabeth Elliott Niedringhaus

CHAPTER

17

As one of the very first readers of *Across the Divide*, I was immediately struck by the distinct clarity describing a number of key "lessons learned" that have defined SSE's success. After several readings, I thought to myself, "We know these principles innately as a management team from working together for so many years, but here they are described and documented so clearly."

This postscript draws attention to five of the lessons that I believe have not only stood the test of time and shaped the fabric of SSE, but will continue to drive SSE's success in the future.

- Staying focused
- Cultivating partners
- Sustaining dedication to community service
- Staying on the technology forefront
- Giving 110 percent

FOCUS, FOCUS, FOCUS

When I became President of SSE in 2004, we had not been achieving top-line growth year-over-year due to the lack of continuity of our purely project-based business model. Adding insult to injury, SSE suffered from unpredictable profitability given the extremely custom nature of our project work. A double whammy!

Bound and determined to change the dynamic of our business model, I convened a meeting of key leaders in SSE to plan for the future. Having just then read Jim Collins' book, *Good to Great,* we naturally dubbed ourselves the Hedgehog Council, as Susan mentioned. Our mission was to determine what we could be the best in the world at, what drove our economic engine and what we were wildly passionate about. The decision, as you have read, was to focus on our business in areas where we could create long-term relationships with our clients so we could consistently deliver value to them as strategic business partners, and generate recurring or "annuity" revenue for SSE.

It seemed impossible in 2004 to make the one decision we probably needed to make, which was to eliminate the services that didn't align with our new business model. At the time, our four services were:

- eLearning
- Network services
- Application development
- Staff augmentation

Hindsight is 20/20, but at the time it seemed to be critically important to keep all lines of our business. Even though two of the four, application development and staff augmentation, didn't fit our strategy, they did provide the necessary cash flow to reinvest in our areas of focus, eLearning and network services.

Over time it became clear that continuing to sell all four lines of our business was distracting us from our primary strategic focus. The turning point for me came upon hearing the then Governor of Louisiana, Bobby Jindal, speak in New Orleans at the 2009 Global Leadership Conference of the Entrepreneurs Organization. Inspired by his message of focus, I returned to St. Louis determined to make the tough decision for SSE. With market forces providing positive reinforcement, we exited the staff augmentation and application development businesses later that year.

It became abundantly clear to me that focus was required to become truly successful at achieving our mission of delivering consistent value to our clients as their strategic business partner. This first lesson of focus is poignantly clear throughout Susan's book as new technologies emerged and/or opportunities arose that threatened to distract SSE's attention and core focus. Remaining focused and refining focus are key ingredients to success.

CLIENTS & EMPLOYEES AS PARTNERS

There is only one truth to relationships with clients and employees: their success is our success!

As evidenced by example after example in Susan's story, doing the right thing by the client has been the foundation of SSE's success and built our long-term client relationships over the span of years and decades. I can hear her refrain today: "It is not important to focus on the money. The money will come if we focus on and take care of the client!"

Likewise, in the realm of employees, the profound success that SSE had out of the gate, as Susan attributed in part to the Independent Contractor (IC) business model, leapt right off the pages at me. The idea that the ICs understood the foundational principles of our business was basic. If the client isn't satisfied and doesn't pay SSE, then there isn't money to pay the contractor.

In the years after we moved away from the IC business model, some of our employees became disconnected from understanding their profound and direct impact on the success of the business. For years, SSE has struggled with the proper way to incentivize our employees and to reinforce their awareness of how they directly impact our success.

Jack Stack's *Great Game of Business* was a perfect case study for me and a model to be leveraged by SSE. As a business person who has learned everything on the job, helping employees learn how to play the game through profit-sharing just made sense to me. Employees have to have "skin in the game." This concept had simply been lost over the years.

While we began this process only a year ago (in 2010), with our senior business leaders in each practice, the impact they have been able to make is amazing with their newly gained insight into our business. We have embarked on a profit-sharing plan for all of our core practices in 2011. In-depth internal education about our business is just beginning. By reconnecting the broken links of knowledge, I anticipate a profound and powerful evolution in our service delivery.

COMMUNITY SERVICE; THROUGH GIVING, YOU RECEIVE

Blessed with many opportunities in her lifetime to give back to the St. Louis region, Susan served the community every time she was asked. As a family, I can remember how often we chided her for taking on yet another responsibility on top of what seemed to be an overflowing plate. I believe St. Louis benefited enormously from her contributions of time, energy and financial resources. Now I realize that SSE also was a profound beneficiary.

In the transition of business leadership, Susan's role as a rainmaker was immediately felt by all at SSE. Day in and day out, she would "make rain" just by being with business leaders at various community and board events and engaging them in conversation. While giving back to our community is simply the right thing to do, it is clear that through giving, you receive!

As a management team today, community engagement is a meaningful part of our corporate life. Whether we are giving back to nonprofits in our community or organizations that impact our professional lines of business, SSE's commitment to community service is unwavering.

STAYING ON THE FOREFRONT OF TECHNOLOGY

When thinking about the company moving forward, there are both constants and variables.

The constants are the very clear principles that have been adapted over time, the foundation of which match Susan's SMOTHER concept:

- Great people are the most valuable asset of the company. We select only the best of the best.
- Each employee takes personal responsibility for his/her work.
- It is easy to do business with us. Common sense and simplicity are our guidelines.
- We do what we say. Our commitments are absolute.
- We contribute to our clients' business success. Their success is our success.
- Our clients love our work and are willing to refer their friends and colleagues. Referrals are the key to our success.

- Our clients write our paychecks each and every week.
- Innovation drives our business.
- We monitor and control our expenses so that we can invest in driving our top-line growth and bottom-line health.
- Recurring revenue is the foundation of our year-over-year growth.
- We win as a team.
- We give back to the community.

The variables are obviously our people, our processes and, most importantly, our technology. The three have a synergistic relationship, but technology is the driver. Our profound challenge again, as Susan has so eloquently defined, is to stay on the cutting edge of technology innovation so clients are willing and happy to pay for our expertise and knowledge to assist them.

The ever-quickening pace of technological change makes this challenge to adapt and innovate as intense as ever. Two key areas to watch are:

- Mobility at our doorstep. We have only just begun to understand the impact mobile technologies will have on our life and how we work. In early 2009, we began to help companies understand how they could leverage mobile platforms to deliver training to their audiences. Mobile Learning (mLearning) is in its infancy, but has enormous promise for delivering training to people "just in time," wherever they are.
- Infrastructure as a commodity. With the advent of virtualization and cloud computing, the infrastructure that supports every business today will continue to become more and more commoditized. Companies' internal IT departments will no longer be required to manage the hardware and software that run their businesses, as maintenance will be purchased as a utility, similar to gas and electricity. The value of technology resources in the organization will be derived from professionals who understand both business and technology. In that dual role, we intend to provide our clients with business leadership to create innovative solutions that improve their operational efficiencies and drive new business offerings.

110 PERCENT

Perhaps the greatest lesson from Susan's story was the clear reminder: if you are going to do something, give it 110 percent. This was a lesson straight from Max De Pree's *Leadership is an Art* that we read as a management team in the early 2000s. I remember this point distinctly touching Susan.

While she had always done this, it seemed that reading De Pree's book was the first time she could label and explain to others what it takes to be successful. As the story goes in the book, if I remember correctly, if you commit to a 95-yard dash to win a race, you have just wasted 95 yards. If your goal is to be the best, then you have to give 110 percent, or don't bother.

Susan's book, like everything else she has ever tackled, is a lesson in 110 percent! At the age of 73 years young, she tackled this book project, bound and determined to be published within a year. Her endeavor has been nothing short of a methodical, tireless commitment of time and energy. But this is no different from how she has lived her entire life, whether learning to cook at the hands of a French chef and writing a cookbook, gardening, teaching a child to read or picking up golf in retirement. This lesson alone is perhaps the greatest gift for anyone to learn!

I am profoundly grateful for the opportunity to learn and grow at the hands of Susan Elliott not only in business, but in life. In business, she has been the greatest inspiration and a cherished role model with her infectious optimism, boundless determination and unwavering ethics. In life as a mother and best friend to me, her constant love, willing ear and consummate encouragement are no doubt the greatest gifts! There are not enough words in the universe to thank her for all she has done for me.

SEVEN SUCCESS CRITERIA

This book shares the stories that express the seven success criteria applied by Susan Elliott to build and sustain her business.

1. **Passion:** Passion for one's initiatives drives commitment and a sense that nothing can stand in the way of success!

2. **Perseverance:** Perseverance is critical to success. Persevere and do not give up if it is something you really want!

3. **Customer Sat(isfaction):** A culture of satisfying clients and exceeding their expectations is imperative; the alternative is a nonstarter!

4. **Integrity:** Impeccable integrity is a given; without it, you have nothing!

5. **People:** People make the real difference! People embrace and communicate the culture; people build the relationships; "people buy from people!"

6. **Focus:** Focus drives expertise, business growth and success!

7. **Change:** "Nothing as constant as change!" My mantra for 50 years!

ACKNOWLEDGEMENTS

This book "journey" has given me the opportunity to make a wonderful new friend, founder and CEO of Casey Communications, Marie Casey, who has guided me through the process from beginning to end. In addition, in computer jargon, she has patiently read and helped make the book "user friendly."

The special friends who took the time to read the manuscript and share their observations in the quotes have helped put the entire book into perspective: I am truly grateful to Jim Denny, Gen. John Handy, Gayle Jackson, Ron Kruszewski, Doug Oberhelman, Fred Salerno, Beth Stroble and Bert Walker.

Others who provided sage advice and assistance from the very beginning to the end of this journey were: Carol Weisman, Sarah Bakewell, Bill Donius and Linda Eardley, who was herself a pioneer as the first woman hired by the *St. Louis Post-Dispatch* to write news. We have been privileged to work with the world-renowned designer, Kiku Obata, as we have through the years, and her colleagues, Amy Knopf and Paul Scherfling. And lastly, our Director of Golf in Florida, Richard A. "Rick" Whitfield, who not only gave me inspiration in tackling golf as a new "project," but also was persistent in urging me to write this story.

As I have stated so many times, we truly appreciate the confidence our clients have placed in SSE and the opportunity to serve their information technology needs. I have always felt a great deal of pride when a client would accept a proposal; it was as if the client reposed trust in me personally, as well as the whole company.

Elizabeth Elliott Niedringhaus, my daughter and now President and CEO of SSE, has successfully assumed the company leadership, so that there is indeed a story to tell. All the rest of the employees through the years are responsible for helping us deliver exceptional service to our clients and perpetuate the culture of SSE. A number of them, both current as well as former colleagues, have participated as "first readers," verifying dates, facts and solution details, as well as offering stories and anecdotes to enrich the message. At the risk of forgetting someone, those who have collaborated include Ellen Bohn, Martha Conzelman, Brenda Enders, Patti Harty, Colin Havard, Kevin Grossnicklaus, Vince Sechrest,

Jill Von Gruben and Susanne White. Two other "first readers," Mary and Frank Rassieur, were helpful in their encouragement and suggestions along the way.

As I have indicated in my list of "Seven Success Criteria" on page 153, it is the people who make the difference: our clients, without whom we would not exist; our employees, who deliver the exceptional service; our outside advisors, who have provided wisdom and advice through the years; and our partners, such as Microsoft, who have been critical components of our service to our clients. In the leadership category, JY Brown joined me in business in 1986 to provide the technical focus that was essential, and Tom Wyman in 2000. Mark Kuhlmann stepped up in 1998 to bring his substantial corporate expertise to SSE for 10 years and provide a bridge to Elizabeth, who became president in 2004 and CEO in 2010.

From a family standpoint, Kathryn Elliott Love is the reason I incorporated SSE in 1966 and she has provided legal advice and great support as our daughter and a board member through the years. My husband, Howard Elliott, Jr., has been my greatest support system and fan from day one and I am eternally grateful for his care and concern. Lastly, of course, we are blessed that Elizabeth came to SSE in 1995 and was inspired by the challenges and opportunities to solve our clients' business problems. She latched onto the significance of technological innovation and change and its importance as a driver to the success of SSE. She is a natural leader and, in my dreams, I could not have imagined any greater success than she has achieved.

My heartfelt thanks and gratitude go to everyone whose lives have touched me and SSE to make this story possible!

— Susan S. Elliott

RELEVANT COMMENTARY

ON WOMEN IN TECHNOLOGY

In an article I wrote for the St. Louis Chapter Data Processing Management Association while at IBM, entitled "Women in Data Processing," I said: "[Women] provide the detailed technical backup for proposal presentations and demonstrations." It was obvious that a direct sales job was not a consideration, and yet the conclusion of the article read: "Wherever there is data processing equipment or a related product or service, today [1964] you are as likely to encounter a woman as a man." George Conrades, an IBM salesman in that era, confirmed IBM could neither complete a sale nor the subsequent implementation without the women because they dotted the i's and crossed the t's to make it a success.

Almost 50 years later, the same issue was reflected in a *New York Times* article on April 18, 2010, entitled, "Out of the Loop in Silicon Valley ... In the Wide-Open World of Tech, So Few Women?" It noted, " ... a stark imbalance of the sexes persists in the high-tech world, where change typically happens at breakneck speed ... substantial barriers still confront women trying to scale the technological peaks."

ON CHANGE & TECHNOLOGY

"Nothing as constant as change" is a given in the technology world. IBM said there were not going to be many computers. No one thought the PC would be the trusted component of corporate business processing; and now the PC is described as vanishing. An article in the *New York Times,* "Computer as Invisible as the Air," published September 5, 2010, reported: "The personal computer is vanishing. Computers once filled rooms, then sat in the closet, moved to our desks, and now nestle in our pockets. Soon the computer may become invisible to us, hiding away in everyday objects ... Thirty–five years ago ... a radical idea that was almost unthinkable: one person, one computer ... In the 1980s, another ... more radical idea: the personal computer, like its predecessor, the mainframe computer ... [would experience] obsolescence ... its successor 'ubiquitous computing' ... is coming true: ... [The 'cloud'] ... Our pens, pads of paper, cars, indeed everything we use are becoming computer smart ... the iPod and Apple TV ... Forecasting what this next-order-of-magnitude increase will mean is impossible."

In the *Wall Street Journal* on March 4, 2011, Apple Inc. CEO Steve Jobs is reported as having declared that the tech industry is in the "post-PC" device era as he introduced the iPad 2.

As mentioned earlier, when I revived SSE in 1983, Lotus 1-2-3 initiated a $1 million advertising campaign to introduce itself, which seemed astronomical at the time. In 2009, Microsoft introduced Bing, its competitor to Google, and "unleashed an advertising campaign estimated to cost $80 million to $100 million." (*New York Times,* "Say Bing," June 7, 2009).

ON PEOPLE IN TECHNOLOGY

In the final analysis, it is the people: the employees, the clients, the advisors and the Microsoft partners of the world that make the difference. People address and interpret change and ultimately provide the continuum for success. They build the relationships with the clients. "People buy from people!" They embrace the culture, one of integrity and the passion for solving business problems with leading-edge technology; they live the culture and communicate it to future generations.

ON BUSINESS MODEL & TECHNOLOGY

Technology teaches us a lesson that we have to heed and respect, in that you have to operate with a business model outside the corporate bureaucratic mold, or it is too costly and cannot accommodate rapid change.

An August 21-22, 2010 article in the *Wall Street Journal,* "The End of Management," validated this concept: "Corporations are bureaucracies ... They are, almost by definition, resistant to change ... Yet in today's world, gale-like market forces – rapid globalization, accelerating innovation, relentless competition ... Even the best managed companies aren't protected from this destructive clash between whirlwind change and corporate inertia ... We have both a need and an opportunity to devise a new form of economic organization ... that can deal with the breakneck realities of the 21st century change. This new model ... will need to be flexible, agile, able to quickly adjust to market developments, and ruthless in reallocating resources to new opportunities ... Change, innovation, adaptability, all have to become orders of the day."

When I went to work for IBM, employees sat in row after row of gray desks; a 180 from SSE, where a new business model was developed on-the-job. It just came naturally! Call it "collaborative" or whatever new definition surfaces, SSE has been using it for 50 years.

IBM began selling its first PCs in a retail environment in 1983-1984. In the "what goes around comes around" category, a December 28, 2010, article in the *Wall Street Journal* described Lenovo's sales growth plan in China. Lenovo bought IBM's PC business in 2005 and "... [it's] using retail franchises who have insight on their individual [emerging] markets and ... first time buyers. In India, [they] aim to add 1,000 franchised retail stores to the 350 it already has."

PC COSTS & FEATURES IN 1981 vs. 2001

VITAL STATISTIC	1981 IBM PERSONAL COMPUTER	2001 DELL OPTIPLEX GX150
Price	$3,045	$1,447
CPU	4.77MHz 8088	933MHz Pentium III
RAM	64KB (.0625MB)	128MB
Storage	160KB floppy drive	20GB hard drive, CD-RW and 1.44MB floppy drives
Display	11.5-inch monochrome text monitor	17-inch, 16.7 million color graphics monitor
Other features	Parallel port, tape cassette port, 2-inch internal speaker	Parallel port, 2 serial ports, 4 USB ports, Ethernet wavetable sound and speakers, microphone jack
Operating system	IBM PC-DOS 1.0	Windows 2000
OS RAM requirements	IBM PC-DOS 1.0	Windows 2000
Boot-up time	16 seconds	51 seconds

GREAT MOMENTS IN PC HISTORY

The evolution of Microsoft Operating Systems beginning with MS-DOS 1.0 in 1981 is chronicled here, prepared by Vince Sechrest, SSE Network Practice Leader.

1981 MS-DOS 1.0

Original version of MS-DOS was released, which was a renamed version of Quick and Dirty Operating System (QDOS) purchased by an upstart company called Microsoft.

1982 MS-DOS 1.25

The PC could read both sides of a floppy disk without turning it over manually.

1983 MS-DOS 2.0

The PC could access 10MB hard disks, directories and double-density 5.25-inch floppy disks with capacities of 360KB.

1983 Netware 68

The first product to bear the Novell NetWare name was released in 1983.

1983 Announcement

Microsoft formally announced Microsoft Windows, a next-generation operating system that would provide a graphical user interface (GUI) and a multitasking environment for IBM computers.

1984 MS-DOS 3.0

The PC could access high-density (1.2MB) floppy disks and 32MB hard disks.

1984 MS-DOS 3.1

Network support was added.

1985 Windows 1.0

Microsoft Windows, version 1.0, released on November 20, 1985, and was originally going to be called Interface Manager, but Rowland Hanson, the head of marketing at Microsoft, convinced the company that the name Windows would be more appealing to consumers. Sale price was $100.

1985 Netware 86

Novell Netware 86 released for Intel 8086.

1986 Netware 286

Novell Netware 286 released to support the Intel 80286 processor.

1987 OS/2 1.0

Microsoft and IBM cooperatively built and released OS/2 1.0.

1987 Windows 2.0

Microsoft Windows version 2.0 was released on December 9, 1987. Much of the popularity for Windows 2.0 came through inclusion of Microsoft's new graphical applications, Excel and Word for Windows.

1989 Netware 386

Novell Netware 386 was released to support the Intel 80386 processor. Later, Novell consolidated the numbering of its NetWare releases, with NetWare 286 becoming NetWare 2.x, and NetWare 386 becoming NetWare 3.x.

1989 Netware 3.0

Novell NetWare 3.0 shipped in the fall of 1989.

1990 Windows 3.0

Microsoft Windows 3.0 was released in 1990.

1991 IBM & Microsoft Split

Following its decision not to develop operating systems cooperatively with IBM, Microsoft changes the name of OS/2 to Windows NT.

1992 Windows 3.1 OS/2 2.0

Microsoft released Windows 3.1 while IBM released OS/2 version 2.0. The IBM/Microsoft competition is under way for control of the PC.

1992 Windows for Workgroups 3.1

Microsoft Windows for Workgroups was the first release to include support for peer-to-peer networking, and allow for easy access to the Internet through corporate networks.

1993 Netware 4.0

NetWare 4.0 was introduced in early 1993.

1993 **Windows NT 3.1**

Microsoft Windows NT 3.1 was released July 27, 1993.

1994 **Windows for Workgroups 3.11**

Microsoft Windows for Workgroups 3.11 was released in February 1994.

1994 **Windows NT 3.5**

Microsoft Windows NT 3.5 was released September 21, 1994.

1995 **Windows NT 3.51**

Microsoft Windows NT 3.51 was released May 30, 1995.

1995 **Windows 95**

Microsoft Windows 95 was released August 24, 1995, and sold more than one million copies within four days.

1996 **Windows NT 4.0**

Microsoft Windows NT 4.0 was released July 29, 1996.

1998 **Windows 98**

Microsoft Windows 98 was released June 1998.

2000 **Windows 2000**

Microsoft Windows 2000 was released February 17, 2000.

2001 **Windows 2001**

Microsoft Windows XP was released October 25, 2001. Bill Gates wanted everyone to have a Windows eXPerience.

2003 **Windows 2003**

Microsoft Windows Server 2003 was released March 28, 2003.

2006 **Windows Vista**

Microsoft Windows Vista was released to corporations on November 30, 2006.

2007 **Windows Vista**

Microsoft Windows Vista was released to the public January 30, 2007.

2008 **Windows Server 2008**

Microsoft Windows Server was released on February 27, 2008.

2009 **Windows 7**

Microsoft Windows 7 was released October 22, 2009.

INDEX

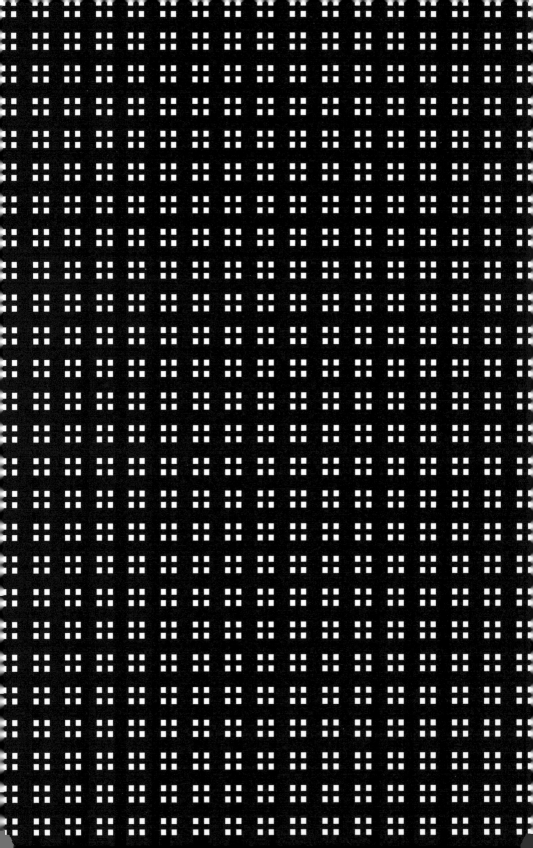